S. HRG. 112–88

# BREAKING THE CYCLE OF NORTH KOREAN PROVOCATIONS

# HEARING

BEFORE THE

## COMMITTEE ON FOREIGN RELATIONS UNITED STATES SENATE

ONE HUNDRED TWELFTH CONGRESS

FIRST SESSION

MARCH 1, 2011

Printed for the use of the Committee on Foreign Relations

Available via the World Wide Web: http://www.fdsys.gov

U.S. GOVERNMENT PRINTING OFFICE

68–240 PDF         WASHINGTON : 2011

For sale by the Superintendent of Documents, U.S. Government Printing Office
Internet: bookstore.gpo.gov  Phone: toll free (866) 512–1800; DC area (202) 512–1800
Fax: (202) 512–2104  Mail: Stop IDCC, Washington, DC 20402–0001

(II)

# CONTENTS

# BREAKING THE CYCLE OF NORTH KOREAN PROVOCATIONS

## TUESDAY, MARCH 1, 2011

U.S. SENATE,
COMMITTEE ON FOREIGN RELATIONS,
*Washington, DC.*

The committee met, pursuant to notice, at 10:09 a.m., in room SD–419, Dirksen Senate Office Building, Hon. John F. Kerry (chairman of the committee) presiding.

Present: Senators Kerry, Lugar, Risch, and Rubio.

## OPENING STATEMENT OF HON. JOHN F. KERRY, U.S. SENATOR FROM MASSACHUSETTS

The CHAIRMAN. Good morning. The hearing will come to order.

I appreciate everybody's patience. I'm sorry to be a couple of minutes late. I appreciate everybody coming, particularly our distinguished witnesses, both of whom could not be more expert, or immersed in and thoughtful about, the subject of North Korea and that part of the world.

I would like to say just a couple quick words, if I can, about events that have been moving at an extraordinary pace in the Middle East during the time that we've been out of session, over the course of the last week or so. Obviously, these demonstrations—these efforts by people to express their will and to find freedom and the capacity to break out of years and years of repression and humiliation—have really changed the world already, no matter what the outcome in each of the individual countries is.

While momentous special events, we've certainly been seeing our own expressions of anger and frustration, whether it's in Wisconsin or in other parts of the country; very different, but, in some ways, their own expression of a frustration with governance, or the absence thereof.

The lesson, however, from the Middle East and the Arab world, is one that I think many of us have anticipated for some period of time, without knowledge of specifically when it might erupt. I had the privilege of speaking at the Islamic Conference in Doha, a year ago, and talked about this question of combined frustration and anger and humiliation that was felt by many people in the streets of Arab countries. Across North Africa and the Middle East, we've now seen people rising up, in a remarkably peaceful way, in pursuit of fundamental human rights and democracy, the freedom to express themselves, and to have a role in choosing the policies that will impact their lives.

We've seen the power of ordinary people to cast off the restraints of autocracies. We've also seen how one individual, used to exercising absolute power, has the ability to delude himself and separate himself from the real interests of his people. And we have seen, in the case of Muammar Gaddafi, a so-called leader who has proven himself to be extraordinarily out of touch with reality and so arrogant in his divorce from reality that he's willing to turn weapons on his own people, not to uphold some larger principle, but simply to reinforce his own personal position and his own personal interests and those of his family.

Colonel Gaddafi has proven himself to be a brutal human being. The United States and its allies, I think, have an enormous responsibility—I think every freedom-loving person on the planet has a responsibility—to side with those who seek to express themselves and to find a different form of government. We have a responsibility to help the Libyan people end four decades of Gaddafi's repressive and, at best, quixotic, extraordinarily mercurial tenure as a so-called leader.

Events that are sweeping the Arab world have powerful implications for America's foreign policy. And one of the things I think we need to make certain is—I'm glad the ships have been deployed, I'm glad that the allies are speaking with one voice, but I don't think we should hesitate to make it clear that if a leader thinks he's simply going to turn mercenaries and powerful secret police on his own people and slaughter them, we have an obligation, as we have in other parts of the world, sometimes met and sometimes not met—I talk of a Bosnia versus a Rwanda—we have an obligation to make ourselves available to make a difference. Whether it's a no-fly zone or some other kind of effort—I think that can tip the balance. And I think that is a critical message, as well as a measure to take, by the United States.

Now, we're here this morning to discuss another part of the world, half a world away from the Middle East, on the Korean Peninsula, where there are also the same kinds of repressive challenges, but even more so because of the threat of nuclear weapons. So, even as we grapple with the crisis of the moment—and there seem to be more and more of them, more frequently—even as we do that, we have an obligation to find the time to deal with other pressing concerns. I don't think there can be any such thing as a back burner, where nuclear weapons and the challenges of a North Korea are concerned.

We need to find a way to break North Korea's cycle—and it is a cycle—of provocation and nuclear expansion, in which they kind of flex their muscles, then move back; they challenge us, we get slightly engaged, something happens, and we go back through the cycle again. That's the way it's been, even as they continue to expand their weaponry and continue to threaten us in other ways by proliferating that weaponry elsewhere in the world.

So, working in concert with South Korea and with Japan, it is a major challenge of the civilized world to persuade North Korea to abandon its reckless behavior and legitimately meet the needs of its people.

We're going to hear first from Assistant Secretary of State for East Asian and Pacific Affairs Kurt Campbell. He was leading a delegation to Christchurch just last week, when the earthquake struck. And I want to take this opportunity, as I know Senator Lugar joins me, in expressing our deepest condolences to all of the folks in New Zealand, and express our best wishes for a speedy recovery. I know this is an enormous challenge. Secretary Campbell was just telling us that it may take as much as 7 percent of their GDP to respond to it. It's an enormous challenge. And we stand with our friends in New Zealand.

Testifying alongside Assistant Secretary Campbell is Ambassador Stephen Bosworth, the administration's special representative for North Korea policy. He's a friend, a constituent of mine, and dean of the Fletcher School of Tufts University.

And we're delighted to see both of you here today.

Last year was the most dangerous in recent memory on the Korean Peninsula, certainly the most dangerous since the end of the Korean war, in 1953. I think we have to do everything within our power to avoid further deterioration and put the Peninsula back on the path to peace and stability. North Korea is making that a hard objective. It's expanded its nuclear and ballistic missile programs in defiance of the U.N. Security Council. It has engaged in reckless attacks on U.S. friend and treaty ally, South Korea. And we must not forget that 46 South Korean seamen died when North Korea sank the *Cheonan,* a year ago; and 4 people were killed later, in the shelling of Yeonpyeong Island.

The U.S. response has been measured, but firm. We've strengthened sanctions and intensified coordination with our key allies, South Korea and Japan. We've also stepped up efforts to convince China to help bring the North back to the negotiating table. So far, international initiatives have not stabilized the situation, much less brought about a change of course in North Korea.

As Asia expert Dr. Victor Cha so aptly put it, "North Korea is the land of lousy options." But, lousy options don't allow us to opt out. Instead, they increase our responsibility to choose policies that will advance our vital national security interests and those of our allies.

And that brings us to today's quandary, and that's the purpose of this hearing. It's been more than 2 years since the last round of the six-party talks on eliminating nuclear weapons on the Korean Peninsula. It's no coincidence that this long silence has been marked by North Korea's dangerous and destabilizing conduct. So, we've all grown weary, if you will, of North Korea's brinkmanship, this habit of ratcheting up the tensions, followed by suggestions of ways to negotiate back from the brink, followed by a few concessions, and then a repetition of the process. I think we need to break this cycle. And we look forward to discussing with our witnesses today: Is that possible? Can one do that? And how do we do it?

The risks of maintaining the status quo, in my judgment, are grave. North Korea is simply going to build more nuclear weapons and missiles. It may well export nuclear technology and fissile material. And the next violation of the armistice could easily escalate into wider hostilities that threaten U.S. allies and interests. So, given these very real risks, the best option is to consult closely with

South Korea and launch bilateral talks with North Korea when we decide the time is appropriate.

Let me make this clear. Fruitful talks between the United States and North Korea could lay the groundwork for the resumption of six-party talks. Right now, we cannot afford to cede the initiative to North Korea and China, because neither country's interests actually fully coincide with ours.

So, let me be clear. We have to get beyond the political talking point that engaging North Korea is somehow "rewarding bad behavior." After all these years, that seems to be an extraordinary canard. It is not rewarding bad behavior. We set the time. We set the place. We can negotiate in good faith. We determine what we're negotiating for. And we never have to say yes to anything that we don't want to. But, if you don't engage in that effort, you have no chance of changing the current dynamic; you actually invite greater instability and greater potential for confrontation.

I believe it's possible to have talks that are based on our national security interests and those of our allies. That's what talking is about. That's what negotiating is about. Nobody forces us to say yes. But, in the absence of that, we don't have a chance of even finding out what it's all about. We don't know what renewed diplomatic engagement can accomplish. We do know this: Our silence invites a dangerous situation to get even more dangerous.

So, finally, I just want to say a quick word about our compelling humanitarian concerns in North Korea. I'm glad that Ambassador Bob King, our special envoy for North Korean human rights issues, could be in the hearing room this morning. Our country has long and wisely separated humanitarian concerns from politics. Consistent with that tradition, we should consider additional food aid to the North. But, that aid needs to be based on a demonstrated need and our ability to verify that food will actually reach the intended recipients. In fact, a broader humanitarian engagement might hold the most long-term promise of unlocking the other puzzles, the nuclear puzzle, enhancing regional peace and security.

And one final comment. When President Hu was here, we discussed this issue and urged him—in fact, asked him the question— why it was not possible for China to take a stronger position to be more engaged in this. And I got a striking answer back that I think they are also finding their patience tried, and are prepared, in fact, to be more engaged, and recognize their own interests, similar to ours, are also at stake. And I think that will be one of the keys to being able to move forward more effectively.

Our first panel is going to be followed by three experts from the private sector: Bob Carlin, a veteran career-watcher with the Center for International Security and Cooperation at Stanford University; Marcus Noland, an economist with the Petersen Institute for International Economics; and Gordon Flake, Northeast Asia expert and executive director of the Mansfield Foundation.

So, again, thank you, both panels, for being here.

Senator Lugar.

### OPENING STATEMENT OF HON. RICHARD G. LUGAR, U.S. SENATOR FROM INDIANA

Senator LUGAR. Well, thank you very much, Mr. Chairman.

I know I express the appreciation of all of your colleagues on this committee for your work during the recess, in Pakistan. We appreciate your stamina and your good counsel there.

Mr. Chairman, we are grateful for the safe return from New Zealand of Assistant Secretary Campbell, Senator and Mrs. Bayh, and others who were in that country at the time of the recent earthquake. Our thoughts and prayers go out to the injured and the families and friends of those who died in this tragic event.

I also want to greet, especially, Ambassador Steve Bosworth. And, as a point of personal privilege, I simply want to recall that we were together 25 years ago, at a time in which President Reagan and Secretary George Shultz, very concerned about the Philippines and the transition there, and the hopes for democracy, asked a delegation, that was headed by the late Jack Murtha and myself, and included you, Mr. Chairman, Senator Cochran of Mississippi, and other business and religious leaders, 26 of us, who fanned out across the islands, under the tutelage and counsel of a very distinguished veteran Ambassador. It was a turning point, in my judgment, for democracy in Asia, and certainly, perhaps, for the world. It stimulated a great deal of interest in our own hemisphere as to what occurred in that momentous time in the Philippines.

So, we welcome you, again, 25 years later, sir. And you're still at it.

Today's hearing will consider ways of dealing with North Korean provocations that have heightened tensions in Northeast Asia. The sinking of a South Korean ship in March 2010, the shelling of South Koreans last November, and the possibility of another nuclear test, illustrate the cycle of North Korean provocations.

In the broader context, today's hearing also provides an opportunity to examine the Obama administration's plan for addressing North Korea's weapons of mass destruction.

In testimony before the Foreign Relations Committee in 2009, Ambassador Bosworth stated, "If North Korea does not heed the unanimous call of the international community and return to negotiations to achieve the irreversible dismantlement of their nuclear and ballistic missile capacity, the United States and our allies in the region will need to take the necessary steps to assure our security in the face of this growing threat."

While the administration has worked closely with South Korea in response to various North Korean provocations during the last 2 years, it is less clear that the administration has developed a strategy with the potential to dismantle North Korea's nuclear weapons program. It is also unclear whether addressing the security threat from North Korea is sufficiently prioritized in our relationship with China. I look forward to the insights of our panels on these questions.

Beyond the disposition of North Korea's nuclear weapons program, the United States and our allies must be devoting great effort to preventing proliferation from North Korea. The North Koreans utilize a network of trading companies to secure components for the North Korean military complex. This web includes as many as 250 trading companies extending to dozens of countries. These same companies reportedly have been used to transfer North Korean nuclear technology to other countries. The risk that sensitive nuclear technology, weapons components, or even weapons themselves, might be transferred out of North Korea for geopolitical objectives or personal profit is an equal, if not greater, threat than North Korea's missile capability.

Instability within the North Korean leadership associated with a transfer of power heightens these concerns, both because of what the regime might do in a time of upheaval, and because individuals facing a purge that could result in loss of personal income may be willing to take greater risks for profit.

The United States and the global community pursue an array of options, hoping to bring about change within North Korea and convince the North Korean Government to eliminate its weapons of mass destruction. Among those measures are economic sanctions. Last year, I requested that the Congressional Research Service assess the status and effectiveness of economic sanctions targeting North Korea, specifically in reference to U.N. Security Council Resolution 1874.

CRS analysts determined that "Implementation has been uneven globally and in cases has diminished over time. An important challenge has been encouraging nations with substantial trade links to North Korea—particularly China, but also a range of nations that serve as transshipment points for North Korean goods, or that have financial institutions that deal with North Korean entities, to implement U.N. sanctions." I invite any of our witnesses to comment on the sanctions situation and provide insight on ways of enhancing sanctions implementation. Mr. Chairman, I will submit the CRS report in its entirety for inclusion in the record of today's hearing.

I am pleased that Ambassador Robert King, the United States Envoy for North Korea Human Rights issues, is in the audience today, as you have mentioned, Mr. Chairman.

I would ask Assistant Secretary Campbell or Ambassador Bosworth to elaborate on Ambassador King's work and how it conforms to the organizational matrix of the administration's North Korea team.

Another point of ongoing interest for me is the POW/MIA issue related to the Korean war. More than 8,000 Americans are listed as missing. Until May 2005, the United States and North Korea cooperated on a recovery program of the remains of United States servicemen. More recently, the United States and China signed a memorandum of understanding so that the United States could receive information on Americans held in China during the Korean war. I am hopeful that the Obama administration will forcefully raise the issue of POWs and MIAs in future communications with North Korea.

The witnesses on our second panel possess remarkable experience and understanding with regard to North Korea. Few Americans have spent as much time on the ground in North Korea as Mr. Carlin. Dr. Noland continues to provide helpful analysis on trends in North Korea's economy and food supply. Mr. Flake has unique perspective on the regional dynamics and implications of events within North Korea. I look forward to their collective assessment of the present situation and recommendations on how we should move forward.

I thank the Chairman.

The CHAIRMAN. Thank you very much, Senator Lugar.

And, without objection, your report will be placed in the record.

[EDITOR'S NOTE.—The CSR report referred to was too voluminous to include in the printed hearing but will be maintained in the permanent record of the committee.]

The CHAIRMAN. Secretary Campbell, we've got two panels, so we want to try to keep matters moving, but thank you again for being here, both of you. We'll go with Secretary Campbell first, and then Ambassador Bosworth.

## STATEMENT OF HON. KURT CAMPBELL, ASSISTANT SECRETARY OF STATE FOR EAST ASIAN AND PACIFIC AFFAIRS, U.S. DEPARTMENT OF STATE, WASHINGTON, DC

Dr. CAMPBELL. Thank you very much, Mr. Chairman and Senator Lugar. It's an honor to be before you today. I want to associate myself with each of your statements and thank you for holding this hearing today.

As you mentioned, Senator Kerry, although the United States is decisively engaged in critical historic developments in the Middle East, it's extraordinarily important for every element of the U.S. Government to send a message to the world that we recognize that we have global interests and that there are critical issues that are playing out in Asia. And the United States remains consequentially involved in these developments. If you look at the 21st century, this will be a region and an era of remarkable opportunity for the United States in Asia. And we must keep our focus in Asia as we go forward, even with dramatic developments playing out in the Middle East.

I want to also say how grateful I am to be here with my friend and colleague Steve Bosworth and Bob King. Unlike occasionally in previous administrations, I think we have tried to approach extraordinarily challenging issues with a very high degree of confidence and collegiality, and I think you will hear that in our testimony today.

I would ask that my full statement be submitted for the record. And I would just very quickly make some opening comments to give you both, and others, the opportunity to ask questions and to perhaps go into details as we go forward.

Let me just also thank both of you for your opening comments about New Zealand. As you indicated, I was with a team of Americans, both on the private side and also government officials, in Christchurch during the devastating earthquake, which has destroyed a large part of this lovely historic city. I have to say, during this tragedy we were able to witness firsthand the remarkable fortitude and courage, and indeed humanity, of the people of New Zealand. And I just want to commit to you both that the U.S. Government will do everything possible to support New Zealand, a country which we are again developing a very strong relationship, in making their way through an enormous challenge, probably the biggest crisis ever to hit New Zealand, in their history.

My primary job today, Senators, is to put the North Korean situation in a larger regional context and give you a sense of how we approach our overall strategy in the Asian-Pacific region. I'll just skim through some of the key elements and principles as we go forward.

I have to just underscore that one of the great benefits of our Asia policy is that we are able to build on a remarkably strong bipartisan consensus about what it takes to be successful in the Asian-Pacific region. I think the Obama administration has recognized that and has sought to build on a succession of successful elements in our overall approach to the Asian-Pacific region.

At the top of that list is continuing to build and maintain very strong bilateral security ties and treaty alliances; and that's with Japan, South Korea, Australia, our friends in Thailand and the Philippines. Currently, I think it would be fair to state that we are enjoying the strongest bilateral relationship that we've ever enjoyed with South Korea. I think our ties are remarkable and that the very strong relationship, both between our two leaders and in our bureaucracies and between our peoples, have allowed us to deal with the extraordinary provocations that you have, I think, rightfully underscored, Senators, when it comes to North Korea.

In addition to these security and political ties, we've also sought to strengthen our overall engagement in Southeast Asia and ASEAN. Clearly that will be a region of growing importance to the United States in the period ahead. We have sought to pursue a consistent and principled engagement with China. At the core of that set of discussions has indeed been North Korea. There are some areas of consensus, and we have had areas of disagreement. We have sought to make a very strong case to China that they need to play a more active role in diplomacy with North Korea, along the lines that you have described.

We are also committed to playing a larger role in the international institutions that are growing in Asia, including the East Asia summit. President Obama will attend the first East Asia summit as a—first East Asia summit of an American leader—later this year, in Bali, in Indonesia.

We're also committed to maintaining a strong and robust military presence in the Asian-Pacific region, that we provide security and stability for a region that is the engine room of the global economy. And that role continues to be essential. And then, frankly, the Asian-Pacific region continues to look at the United States as a key player in the economy and the macroeconomic issues in the Asian-Pacific region.

We are committed to engaging openly and consistently in the trade agenda of Asia. I think, as you know, we will be submitted, shortly, the Korea Free Trade Agreement for consideration to the U.S. Congress. And obviously, we are involved in very consequential diplomacy associated with the TPP, which will be, if successful, one of the most important trade agreements in Asia in many years.

These form the overall basis of our approach to Asia.

And I must say that, despite the tremendous opportunities that we see in Asia, that have become part of our popular discourse, one country, indeed, stands out as an outlier—and, in fact, an impediment—to the region's promising future: the DPRK, North Korea. And the DPRK's brazen attack on the South Korean corvette *Cheonan,* which you have both referred to, in March of last year, its recent disclosure of a uranium enrichment program, its shelling of Yeonpyeong Island, with civilians stationed there, that resulted in a large loss of South Korean life, coupled with the *Cheonan* sinking and its ongoing human rights violations, underscore the threat that North Korea's policies and provocations, including its nuclear and ballistic missile programs and proliferation activities, pose to regional stability and, indeed, global security.

We are committed to addressing these issues through an active and determined diplomacy, using all elements of our policy at our disposal, with all the parties involved.

You stated at the outset, Senator Kerry, that our goal must be to break the cycle. And that is, indeed, what the United States is determined to do.

I look forward to exploring the various elements that each of you have laid out in your opening statements in the discussion subsequently.

Thank you both very much.

[The prepared statement of Dr. Campbell follows:]

PREPARED STATEMENT OF DR. KURT M. CAMPBELL

Chairman Kerry, Senator Lugar, and members of the committee, thank you for inviting me to testify today on North Korea, one of our most enduring foreign policy challenges. I would also like to personally thank this committee for its leadership in advancing discussion and opportunities for American engagement in the Asia-Pacific region. Today, I would like to use this occasion to focus on the administration's North Korea policy through a broader regional context.

INTRODUCTION

The primary strategic objective for U.S. engagement in the Asia-Pacific region is to promote a peaceful and stable security environment that advances the interests of the United States, our allies, and partners in the region. Essential to this approach is the security and stability that our alliances with Japan, the Republic of Korea (ROK), Australia, Thailand, and the Philippines provide. These relationships underwrite peace and security in the region and provide a context for the region's tremendous economic dynamism and vitality. In addition, our alliances are buttressed by a network of partnerships ranging from Indonesia to New Zealand and an evolving regional political and security architecture that will help create rules of the road for this rapidly evolving and strategically critical region. China is also a key U.S. partner in promoting peace and security in the Asia-Pacific region and globally, and the joint statement issued during President Hu's January 2011 to Washington underscored that "in coordination with other parties, the United States and China will endeavor to increase cooperation to address common concerns and promote shared interests."

Despite the tremendous opportunities in Asia that have become part of our popular discourse, one country stands out as an outlier, and in fact an impediment, to the region's promising future: the Democratic People's Republic of Korea's (DPRK). The DPRK's brazen attack on the ROK corvette *Cheonan* in March of last year, its recent disclosure of a uranium enrichment program, its shelling of Yeonpyong Island that resulted in the tragic loss of South Korean lives, and its ongoing human rights violations underscore the threat that the DPRK's policies and provocations, including its nuclear and ballistic missile programs and proliferation activities, pose to regional stability and global security.

The verifiable denuclearization of the Korean Peninsula, which is the core objective of the 2005 joint statement of the six-party talks, is an essential ingredient to the Asia-Pacific region's long-term success and to our own security. Progress toward this goal requires close coordination between the ROK, Japan, and the United States, as well as with China and Russia. Our Northeast Asian alliances play an essential role in maintaining regional security, deterring North Korean provocations, providing a reliable and robust strategic deterrent posture, and bringing maximum leverage to bear on the DPRK to change its current course and become a member of the community of nations. To this end, we have actively engaged our regional partners to ensure robust implementation of U.N. Security Council Resolutions (UNSCR) 1718 and 1874 on North Korea, and though there is still work to be done, strong regional cooperation, particularly with Japan and South Korea, has made it more difficult for North Korea to successfully engage in proliferation and other illicit activities. We will continue to take steps to enhance and broaden our bilateral political, economic, and security relations, as well as make progress on key alliance modernization initiatives. We will also work to develop a more integrated trilateral framework for cooperation and coordination between Seoul, Tokyo, and Washington. Furthermore, we are taking steps to enhance coordination with China and Russia—both of which have important relationships with North Korea—to create a more favorable context for denuclearization and peace and security. In addition to the aforementioned five key parties, we are working more closely with other stakeholders like the Association of Southeast Nations (ASEAN), India, and Australia to broaden regionwide efforts to compel North Korea to abide by its denuclearization commitments and obligations, as well as with the U.N. Security Council.

*The Republic of Korea*

The United States-ROK alliance is grounded in the threat that North Korea poses to the ROK. However, over the course of the past few years, the United States has undertaken steps to expand alliance cooperation in both regional and global settings. In 2011, we will aggressively pursue initiatives to increase collaboration in the peninsular, regional, and global contexts.

The ROK's security is critically affected by North Korea due to their complex historical relationship, geographic proximity, and the tangible threat that North Korea's conventional military capabilities, nuclear programs, and ballistic missile developments pose to South Korea. As President Obama stated during his November 2010 visit to Seoul, "In the face of these threats, the U.S.-ROK alliance has never been stronger . . . The United States will never waver in our commitment to the security of the Republic of Korea." Following the attack on Yeonpyong Island, President Obama stated that we will stand "shoulder to shoulder" with the ROK and reaffirmed our commitment to its defense. This commitment is being translated through efforts to bolster ROK defensive capabilities. For example, last November the ROK participated in USS *George Washington* carrier group exercises. We continue to hold regular joint military exercises to enhance extended deterrence, interoperability, and the readiness of alliance forces to respond to threats to peace.

Over the last 60 years, our alliance with the ROK has continued to expand from its military roots into one of the most vibrant, full-spectrum strategic partnerships in modern history, encompassing dynamic political, economic, and social cooperation. The U.S.-Korea Free Trade Agreement is a way not only to strengthen United States-ROK economic ties and increase American jobs through exports to Korea but also to enhance the enduring strength of this strategic relationship. Regionally, we are working closely with the ROK on a number of key issues, such as improving maritime security through the ASEAN Regional Forum and advancing the capacities of countries in the Lower Mekong region. We welcome and support the ROK Government's efforts to realize its "Global Korea" vision, expanding its global reach to be commensurate with its economic status. We applaud the ROK's leadership in addressing global concerns, such as proliferation, counterpiracy, and development assistance. Last year's G20 summit in Seoul and the upcoming Nuclear Security Summit in Seoul in 2012 are a testament to the ROK's global leadership.

Close coordination and the broadening and deepening of our security commitments with the ROK are key guiding principles for how we approach North Korea. The steps that our two militaries are taking, for example, to enhance our joint interoperability and strategic deterrent, are critical to creating a security environment that deters North Korean provocations, increases our collective leverage on Pyongyang to change course, and maintains peace and stability in the broader East Asia environment. A United States-ROK relationship that will only grow stronger and continued close bilateral coordination on our strategies for the way forward on North Korea will reinforce our common message to Pyongyang—that taking irreversible steps toward denuclearization, abiding by the terms of the Armistice Agreement, and improving relations with the ROK and its other neighbors is the only way for the DPRK to break free from its isolation and enjoy the security, political, and economic benefits that come with integrating into the international community.

In the short-term, the United States supports direct talks between the DPRK and the ROK to address the South's legitimate grievances, including North Korea's sinking of the *Cheonan* and its shelling of Yeonpyong Island. We believe that North-South dialogue is an important initial step toward the resumption of the six-party talks. North Korea's decision to walk out of the recent colonel-level North-South military-to-military talks squandered a valuable opportunity to improve North-South relations and demonstrate its commitment to dialogue. We will carefully monitor events on the Korean Peninsula for evidence of a North Korean commitment to improving inter-Korean relations.

*Japan*

President Obama underscored the importance of the United States-Japan alliance during his November 2010 trip to Japan: "As allies for over half a century, the partnership between Japan and the United States has been the foundation for our security and our prosperity—not only for our two countries, but also for the region." Last year, we celebrated the 50th anniversary of the United States-Japan alliance. This year, we are working to create a roadmap for the next 50 years to broaden and deepen this cornerstone alliance. In this context, Secretaries Clinton and Gates will cohost their Japanese counterparts in Washington, DC, for a 2+2 Security Consultative Committee meeting. This meeting will focus on reaffirming the core mission of our alliance—the security of Japan and maintaining peace and security in the Asia-Pacific—as well as articulating new common strategic objectives and approaches that demonstrates the expanse of our relationship. Progress on key issues associated with modernizing our military relationship will continue and is essential to adapt our alliance to better manage the complex evolutions in the Asia-Pacific strategic environment, as well as promote and protect the global commons. We think that Japan should follow the ROK and take steps to accede to the Hague Convention on International Parental Child Abduction.

North Korea remains Japan's most immediate national security concern and a key feature of our diplomatic engagement with Tokyo. North Korea's nuclear and ballistic missile programs and past abduction of Japanese citizens underscore the tangible threat the DPRK poses to Japan's national security. North Korea's recent provocative actions have reinforced Japan's concerns and led to enhanced ROK-Japan cooperation and closer trilateral U.S.-ROK-Japan coordination. We welcome the commitment of ROK and Japanese leaders to deepen the ROK-Japan bilateral relationship. We appreciate Japan's key role in working to resolve the North Korea nuclear issue peacefully and its commitment to implementing unilateral and multilateral sanctions against the DPRK to curb its proliferation activities. The United States fully supports Japanese efforts to resolve the issue of Japanese citizens abducted by North Korea.

*Trilateral U.S.-ROK-Japan Coordination*

In addition to strengthening U.S. alliances with the ROK and Japan, we will take ambitious steps to increase trilateral cooperation to further develop a more integrated Northeast Asia security architecture. Robust trilateralism is essential to deal with the DPRK's provocative behavior and to shape the emerging regional strategic environment. Trilateral engagement demonstrates to North Korea that its reckless actions will be met with collective resolve. The benefits of trilateral coordination were on full display when Secretary Clinton hosted Japanese Foreign Minister Maehara and ROK Foreign Minister Kim in a historic United States-Japan-ROK Trilateral Ministerial meeting in December 2010. At this meeting, the three countries jointly affirmed the importance of unity and ways to enhance policy coordination on myriad issues from ASEAN to North Korea. On North Korea, they declared that the DPRK's belligerent actions threaten all three countries and will be met with solidarity from all three countries. The United States reaffirmed its security alliances with both Japan and the ROK, and all three countries jointly condemned the DPRK's uranium enrichment facility as a violation of the DPRK's commitments under the September 2005 joint statement of the six-party talks and its obligations under UNSCR 1718 and 1874. Institutionalization of trilateral cooperation will be an important focus of U.S. diplomatic efforts in the coming year and a point of conversation when Secretary Clinton meets with the ROK and Japanese Foreign Ministers in the coming year. Additionally, with our Japanese and South Korean allies, we are continually working to enhance cooperation with China and Russia on ways to deal with the DPRK—underscoring the strategic benefits of strong five-party unity and coordination in denuclearization negotiations.

*China*

North Korea remains a key foreign policy issue in our bilateral relationship with China. We share the same goals of peace and stability on the Korean Peninsula, as well as North Korea's verifiable denuclearization in a peaceful manner. China is uniquely positioned to influence the DPRK because of its significant economic and humanitarian aid to the DPRK, its shared border with the DPRK, and historical ties. We have urged China to press North Korea to take appropriate steps to improve relations with South Korea and to denuclearize. We also continue to work with China to enhance effective implementation of sanctions under UNSCR 1718 and 1874.

During the January 2011 China state visit, President Obama emphasized to President Hu that North Korea's nuclear and ballistic missile programs are increasingly a direct threat to the security of the United States and our allies. The President also expressed appreciation for China's role in reducing tensions on the Korean Peninsula but underscored the need for China to leverage its unique relationship with North Korea to compel Pyongyang to abide by its commitment to the 2005 joint statement of the six-party talks as well as its obligations under UNSCR 1718 and 1874. Both leaders agreed that the complete denuclearization of the Korean Peninsula remains our paramount goal and that North Korea must avoid further provocations.

The joint statement issued during President Hu's visit also reflects our shared concern over the DPRK's claimed uranium enrichment program. The United States and China jointly "expressed concern regarding the DPRK's claimed uranium enrichment program . . . opposed all activities inconsistent with the 2005 joint statement and relevant international obligations and commitments . . . and . . . called for the necessary steps that would allow for the early resumption of the six-party talks process to address this and other relevant issues." We are working closely with China and our other partners and allies at the U.N. to develop an appropriate U.N. response to the DPRK's uranium enrichment program.

*Russia*

We value our continuing cooperation with Russia, another key partner in the six-party talks, to achieve our shared goal of denuclearization in North Korea. As a result of its historical relationship with the DPRK and its status as a Permanent Member of the U.N. Security Council, like China, Russia is well positioned to influence the DPRK through both direct bilateral diplomacy and multilateral efforts.

In the wake of the DPRK's provocations over the last year, we welcome the constructive role that Russia has played to press Pyongyang to refrain from further destabilizing actions, to abide by its international commitments and obligations, and to take irreversible steps toward denuclearization. Russia has publicly stated that it backs U.N. Security Council discussion of the North Korean uranium enrichment program, and we seek further cooperation from Russia in our efforts to affirm unequivocally that the DPRK's uranium enrichment activities violate the relevant UNSCR.

*Other Key Regional Players: ASEAN, India, Australia*

Due to the security threats posed by North Korea to the entire Asia-Pacific region, our deep diplomatic activity and coordination on North Korea extend beyond the five parties to other key partners in the region. As a fulcrum of regional multilateralism, ASEAN has been actively engaged on regional security issues. The ASEAN-centered East Asia summit presents a unique opportunity to engage with traditional allies and new partners on a range of areas central to U.S. interests in Asia, which may grow to include North Korea. We will continue to work closely with ASEAN to identify ways for the organization to play a more engaged role in denuclearization discussions.

India and Australia also share our goal of enhancing peace and security in the Asia-Pacific. The United States and India have discussed North Korea in our Strategic Dialogue and other bilateral and multilateral exchanges. India's growing security and political relations with Japan and South Korea will also enhance prospects for security and stability in Northeast Asia. Australia has strongly supported international implementation of UNSCR 1718 and 1874, participated in the international investigation of the sinking *Cheonan,* and supported efforts to bring the issue before the U.N. Security Council.

CONCLUSION

The goal of the United States and our allies and partners remains a stable, peaceful Korean Peninsula free of nuclear weapons. To achieve this goal, the United States intends to maintain strong solidarity with South Korea, Japan, and other states with a vested interest in the future of the Korean Peninsula and the stability and prosperity of Northeast Asia. We will continue to encourage the DPRK to engage in meaningful negotiations on denuclearization and to honor its commitments and international obligations. At the same time, we will work to ensure the implementation of U.S. and international sanctions against North Korea's nuclear, missile, and proliferation networks and its involvement in other illicit activities. We will also carefully watch internal political and economic developments in North Korea, particularly as they relate to succession and the promotion of heir apparent Kim Jong-un, the third son of Kim Jong-il.

The Obama administration has repeatedly stressed that there remains a positive path open to North Korea. North Korea has the choice to take a path that will lead to security and economic opportunity or to continue in its pattern of confrontation and isolation. The United States remains committed to meaningful dialogue, but we will not reward North Korea for shattering the peace or defying the international community. If North Korea improves relations with South Korea and demonstrates a change in behavior, including taking irreversible steps to denuclearize, complying with international law, and ceasing provocative behavior, the United States will stand ready to move toward normalization of our relationship. However, if it maintains its path of defiance and provocative behavior and fails to comply with its obligations and commitments, it stands no chance of becoming a strong and prosperous nation.

Our concerns with North Korea are not limited to the threat it poses to regional stability and global security. Human rights violations harm the North Korea people and violate international norms for the rule of law and respect for individual rights. Respect for human rights by North Korea will also be necessary for it to fully participate in the international community. Human rights are a top U.S. priority and an addressing of human rights issues by the DPRK will have a significant impact on the prospect for closer United States-DPRK ties.

Thank you for the opportunity to appear before you today and I welcome any questions that you may have.

The CHAIRMAN. Thank you, Secretary.

Mr. Ambassador.

## STATEMENT OF HON. STEPHEN W. BOSWORTH, SPECIAL REPRESENTATIVE FOR NORTH KOREA POLICY, U.S. DEPARTMENT OF STATE, WASHINGTON, DC

Ambassador BOSWORTH. Thank you very much, Mr. Chairman, Senator Lugar. It's a pleasure to be here with you, both of you, this morning. And I look forward to a useful exchange of views and will try very hard to respond to all of your questions.

The CHAIRMAN. Can you pull the mic a little closer, please?

Ambassador BOSWORTH. Sure.

The CHAIRMAN. Thanks.

Ambassador BOSWORTH. Is that better?

The CHAIRMAN. Yes.

Ambassador BOSWORTH. Oh, yes. Sorry. [Laughter.]

I would just, to sort of introduce this subject, supplement the prepared statement that has been submitted and say that the United States has been struggling with the issue of nuclear weapons in North Korea for the past 25 years. There have been times when we have made some progress, only, unfortunately, to see it largely slip away. We have been able to deal with its provocations, but North Korea poses an enduring challenge to U.S. interests in the region and the interests of all other countries in the region.

They are a pole of instability in the heart of what is arguably the most important economic region of the world today. They are also, of course, a major threat to American and other norms regarding proliferation of nuclear weapons. So, this is a challenge that must be dealt with. We do not have the option, in my judgment, of simply biding our time and ignoring them.

In response to the provocations which Kurt Campbell has described, what we have pursued is essentially a two-track policy. On the one hand, working very closely with our allies and our partners in the six-party talks, we have, through the United Nations and bilaterally, tightened our sanctions on North Korea. It is difficult to measure the exact effect of those sanctions, but this is something we work at every day. We are constantly coordinating with all of the partners in the North—in the six-party process to ensure that the sanctions achieve maximum effectiveness. And I think there is no question that the sanctions have made life more complicated and more difficult for the DPRK.

At the same time, however, we recognize that sanctions are not, in and of themselves, a full policy toward this problem. So, we have remained, and will remain, open to constructive dialogue. And we view diplomacy, ultimately, as the best way of solving these difficulties in this challenge.

We have been in constant coordination with our partners in the region, particularly with South Korea and Japan, but also with China and Russia. We are engaged in efforts to make sure that, on the one hand, the sanctions remain effective, tightened, and, on the other hand, to demonstrate that we are serious about the use of diplomacy, but serious in the sense that we want assurance that North Korea regards these prospective talks seriously. We are not interested in talking just for the sake of talking. We want talks which produce concrete results. We remain committed, as do our other partners in the six-party process, at least South Korea, Japan, China, and Russia, to full implementation of the agreed statement—the joint statement of September 2005, which pledged continued concentration on nonproliferation and other elements to bring about stability on the Korean Peninsula.

On the subject of food aid, which has been raised earlier, we continue to pursue a longstanding U.S. policy on food aid. We do separate humanitarian assistance from political issues, but we provide food aid when we see a perceived need and in a situation in which we can monitor how the food aid is used, who are the recipients of that food aid, and does it go to the people for whom we intend it.

On the subject of human rights and other humanitarian issues, I am very pleased to be working very closely with my friend and colleague, Bob King, who is part of our office. We talk frequently and closely coordinate on all issues. Bob has just returned from an extended trip to South Korea, where subjects, including North Korean human rights performance, food aid, the general situation on the Korean Peninsula, in North Korea, have been very prominent on his agenda. So, I think that this relationship gives evidence of the fact that, as we approach the problems of North Korea and the challenges that it poses, we are very concerned about human rights and we are very concerned about the condition of the North Korean people.

So, I will stop there and, like my friend Kurt Campbell, make myself available for your questions.

Thank you.

[The prepared statement of Ambassador Bosworth follows:]

PREPARED STATEMENT OF HON. STEPHEN W. BOSWORTH

Chairman Kerry, Senator Lugar, and members of the committee, thank you for inviting me to testify today on Democratic People's Republic of Korea (DPRK). The North Korea issue is one of the most important foreign policy challenges of our time. North Korea's nuclear and ballistic missile program and proliferation activity pose an acute threat to a region of enormous economic vitality as well as to our global nonproliferation efforts and to our security interests more generally.

North Korea has repeatedly reneged on its commitments under the September 2005 joint statement made in the context of the six-party talks. It has also failed to comply with a number of U.N. Security Council Resolution (UNSCR) obligations. At the beginning of his administration, President Obama expressed a willingness to engage North Korea. It responded by conducting missile tests, expelling IAEA inspectors, announcing a nuclear test, disclosing its uranium enrichment program, and stating that the six-party talks were "dead." It also expelled the U.S. personnel delivering food aid to the North Korean people. The United States has been a leader of a unified international response to these North Korean provocations. The U.N. Security Council adopted UNSCRs 1718 and 1874, calling on North Korea to immediately cease its nuclear activities and provocative actions.

North Korea's provocative actions have continued this past year, with its sinking of the Republic of Korea (ROK) corvette *Cheonan* in March and its artillery attack of South Korean Yeonpyong Island in November. The United Nations Security Council issued a strong statement condemning the attack which lead to the sinking of the *Cheonan.*

Following the attack on Yeonpyong Island, President Obama reaffirmed our commitment to the defense of the ROK and emphasized that we will stand "shoulder to shoulder" with our ally. The United States continues to demonstrate our commitment to deter North Korean provocations through joint military exercises with the ROK. For instance, the ROK participated in the November 27–30 USS *George Washington* carrier group exercises. We also continue to strengthen our nonproliferation efforts with regard to North Korea, including the adoption of new unilateral sanctions targeting DPRK illicit activities.

We strongly believe that North-South dialogue that takes meaningful steps toward reducing inter-Korean tensions and improving relations should precede a resumption of the six-party talks. We believe North-South talks are an important opportunity for North Korea to demonstrate its sincerity and willingness to engage in dialogue. Ultimately, if North Korea fulfills its denuclearization commitments, the Five Parties are prepared to provide economic assistance and help to integrate North Korea into the international community.

In November, North Korea disclosed a uranium enrichment program and claimed that it was building a light-water nuclear reactor. These activities clearly violate North Korea's commitments under the 2005 joint statement and its obligations under UNSCRs 1718 and 1874. The United States is working with Japan, South Korea, and the UNSC to make clear that its Uranium Enrichment Program is prohibited by its commitments and obligations to UNSC resolutions 17818 and 1874 and the 2005 joint statement.

Looking into the future, we continue to firmly believe that a dual-track approach to North Korea offers the best prospects for achieving denuclearization and a stable region. We are open to meaningful engagement but will continue to pursue the full and transparent implementation of sanctions. We are looking for demonstrable steps by North Korea that it is prepared to meet its international obligations and commitments to achieve the goal of the 2005 joint statement: the verifiable denuclearization of the Korean Peninsula in a peaceful manner.

In the meantime, the United States is continuing to consult closely with our partners in the six-party process. President Obama and Secretary Clinton have been at the forefront of this effort, reaching out to leaders in Japan, South Korea, China, and Russia. In early January, I led an interagency delegation to the Republic of Korea, China, and Japan. In all three capitals, I met with senior government officials to discuss next steps on the Korean Peninsula. I was accompanied by special envoy for the six-party talks, Sung Kim, who coordinates U.S. efforts on the six-party talks and leads day-to-day engagement with six-party partners.

During a mid-January visit to the United States by PRC President Hu Jintao, we made progress on greater cooperation with the Chinese on North Korea issues. In a joint statement issued during the visit, both sides agreed that the complete denuclearization of the Korean Peninsula remains our paramount goal. The United States and China also jointly "expressed concern regarding the DPRK's claimed uranium enrichment program," "opposed all activities inconsistent with the 2005 joint statement and relevant international obligations and commitments," and "called for the necessary steps that would allow for the early resumption of the six-party talks process to address this and other relevant issues."

Immediately following this visit in late January, Deputy Secretary Steinberg led a mission to Seoul, Tokyo, and Beijing to further coordinate our approach to the Korean Peninsula.

In addition, we have further solidified our alliances with the ROK and Japan and have improved trilateral cooperation among the three countries in responding to the DPRK's provocative and belligerent behavior. For example, at the December 6, 2010, U.S.-Japan-ROK Trilateral Ministerial meeting, Secretary Clinton, Japanese Foreign Minister Maehara, and ROK Foreign Minister Kim affirmed unity among the three nations and declared that the DPRK's provocative and belligerent behavior threatens all three countries and will be met with solidarity from all three countries.

In the meantime, the United States continues to improve the implementation of unilateral and international sanctions on North Korea to constrain its nuclear and missile programs. On August 30, the President signed Executive Order (E.O.) 13551, giving the U.S. Government new authorities to target North Korea's conventional arms proliferation and illicit activities. The new E.O. designated one North Korean individual and five North Korean entities. The Departments of State and Treasury also recently designated five additional entities and three individuals under existing E.O. 13382, which targets North Korean WMD-related proliferation activities. We continue to urge the international community to implement UNSCRs 1718 and 1874 fully and transparently. At the same time, we have stated unequivocally that we will not lift sanctions on the DPRK just for their returning to talks.

In March 2009, the DPRK terminated the U.S. food aid program, ordering our humanitarian personnel out of the country and requiring that they leave behind 20,000 metric tons of undelivered U.S. food items. The United States remains deeply concerned about the well-being of the North Korean people, particularly in light of continuing reports of chronic food shortages. The U.S. Government policy on humanitarian assistance and food aid is based on three factors: (1) level of need; (2) competing needs in other countries; and (3) our ability to ensure that aid is reliably reaching the people in need. This policy is consistent with our longstanding goal of providing emergency humanitarian assistance to the people of countries around the world where there are legitimate humanitarian needs. However, consistent with our practices worldwide, the United States will not provide food aid without a thorough assessment of actual needs and adequate program management, monitoring, and access provisions to ensure that food aid is not diverted or misused.

The United States also remains deeply concerned about the human rights situation in North Korea. We work closely with the United Nations, including the Human Rights Council, other international and nongovernmental organizations, and other governments to try to improve the human rights situation in North Korea. The State Department's 2009 Country Report on Human Rights Practices for North Korea reports that the DPRK Government continued to commit numerous serious abuses. Advancing human rights is a top U.S. priority in our North Korea policy. Any long-term improvement in U.S.-DPRK relations will be contingent, among several factors, on the DPRK making a serious effort to address human rights issues. Special Envoy for North Korean Human Rights Issues Robert King traveled to South Korea in early February to meet with South Korean Government officials, as well as North Korean defectors, civil society groups, and North Korea experts. Ambassador King reports from his meetings that North Korea's human rights and humanitarian situation continues to worsen.

We are also working closely with the U.N. and other organizations to protect North Korean refugees. The United States has urged China to adhere to its international obligations as a party to the 1951 Refugee Convention and its 1967 Protocol, including by not expelling or refouling North Koreans protected under those treaties and undertaking to cooperate with UNHCR in the exercise of its functions. Although the vast majority of North Korean refugees choose resettlement in the ROK, the United States will consider resettling eligible North Korean refugees who express an interest in resettlement to the United States directly to U.S. Embassies and consulates or through the United Nations High Commissioner for Refugees (UNHCR). We support increasing the flow of balanced information into the DPRK through independent broadcasters based in the ROK and in collaboration with the Broadcasting Board of Governors and its partners Voice of America and Radio Free Asia. The United States considers remains recovery operations to be an important humanitarian mission. We remain committed to achieving the fullest possible accounting for U.S. POW/MIAs from the Korean war, as well as from other conflicts.We are also carefully watching internal developments in North Korea, particularly as they relate to leadership succession and the promotion of heir apparent, Kim Jong-un, the youngest son of Kim Jong-il, to key regime positions. In conclusion, we continue to work closely with our six-party partners in an effort to promote peace and stability on the Peninsula and achieve the goals of the 2005 six-party joint statement. We believe we can make progress in cooperation with our partners in Tokyo, Beijing, Moscow, and Seoul. We are also working with our partners and the United Nations to advance human rights in North Korea, protect the status of North Korean refugees, and monitor the need for humanitarian assistance in North Korea. The door is open to Pyongyang to join and benefit from such an effort but only if it abandons the misguided notion that violence, threats, and provocation are the path toward achievement of its goals.

We face enormous challenges when dealing with North Korea. The denuclearization of the Korean Peninsula will not be easy to achieve, but we cannot abandon the goal. Through a strategy that combines openness to dialogue with a continuation of bilateral and multilateral sanctions, we believe we have an opportunity to bring about important improvements to the global nonproliferation regime and to regional and global security. We believe that our partners in the six-party process share this assessment and we will continue to work closely with them as we move forward.

Thank you for the opportunity to appear before you today. I welcome any questions you may have.

The CHAIRMAN. Thank you very much, Ambassador, and thanks for your continued service in this regard.

Let me try to probe this thing a little bit, get underneath, if we can, what you've been talking about, in terms of the efforts to strengthen our initiatives.

Mr. Secretary, some people suggest—you know they're the—sort of these polar opposites: isolate them, don't talk to them, basically let the regime collapse by bringing all this external pressure on them, and then hopefully, there's something new to get engaged with; versus, you know, getting engaged now, going along with this cycle of concessions, which you can't distinguish before the talks whether it is going to occur or not. I mean, you just said, Mr. Ambassador, we don't want to talk to them for the sake of talking, but, I mean, they can come to us and say, "Hey, we're really ready. Yes, we'll sit down. Let's go talk. We'll go through this. We're absolutely prepared to get good results." They're not going to serve up the results until you have talked, correct? So, you're going to have to go through some kind of measure of testing whether or not it's real.

Ambassador BOSWORTH. I think that's correct. I mean, one of the things that we are looking for, however, is evidence that the agreements that we have reached with them in the past are agreements which they are now prepared to carry out.

The CHAIRMAN. Do you want that evidence in terms of their adhering to the agreement, or saying they will?

Ambassador BOSWORTH. Well, we want evidence that they treat these things seriously and that they are not making agreements just for the sake of getting talks started. We want to see concrete results.

The CHAIRMAN. Does that——

Ambassador BOSWORTH. We also——

The CHAIRMAN. Does that put a hurdle in the way of getting to the other talks?

Ambassador BOSWORTH. No, I don't believe it does.

The CHAIRMAN. What if they think that's part of the bargain?

Ambassador BOSWORTH. Well, these are agreements they've already made. It's very difficult to go forward with confidence and make new agreements if they are not able to adhere to the ones that we've already put in place.

The CHAIRMAN. And if they're not, do you give a deadline? Is there a greater capacity to bring pressure on them to go the regime-collapse route?

Ambassador BOSWORTH. Well, I'm not very confident about regime collapse as a route toward stability on the Korean Peninsula. One can argue that we've been waiting for that regime to collapse for a long time, and it's still there. No, I think we have to deal with

North Korea as we find it, not as we would like it to be perhaps at some point in the future.

The CHAIRMAN. Let me go further than that, if I can, for a moment, both of you. Isn't it fair to say that regime collapse is distinctly against China's interests?

Dr. CAMPBELL. I would say so, Senator. In fact, I think one of the things that has animated China's positions on North Korea in recent years has been a concern about stability in North Korea. And they have taken steps to strengthen their ties militarily, at the party level, and economically with the regime's elite. I think it would be fair to say, though, that, in some of our discussions with our Chinese interlocutors, they, too, have expressed concerns about developments in North Korea.

The CHAIRMAN. But, this doesn't break us through yet. I mean, my frustration, a little bit, is that they keep paying lipservice to the notion that North Korea's activities are threatening, and they don't want them to be an expansive nuclear power, and they don't want them to proliferate, but then they keep throwing this very traditional Chinese concern about stability—I think, partly because of their own internal politics and partly because of what the impact would be on them, of refugees and collapse and other things.

So, there's a tension here. We just don't get beyond that. And the question is whether or not you think China is prepared to get beyond it. It seems to me China—if China wanted to flex a little muscle here—could have a profound impact on what North Korea's attitude is about its future.

Ambassador BOSWORTH. Well, clearly, China has enormous interest in North Korea, in general. I am convinced that we share one large common interest between the United States and China, and that is that neither of us want to see North Korea as a nuclear-weapon state on an ongoing basis.

North Korea is also, as you point out, Mr. Chairman, very concerned about stability in North Korea; stability in Northeast Asia, in general. And it is, I think, obvious that there are, at times, understandable tensions between their objective of denuclearization and their objective of reducing or avoiding serious tension on the peninsula.

We work with China on this issue on an ongoing basis. I've made, since I've been in this position, about seven trips to Beijing. The Chinese have come here. It is a subject of primary tension when our two Presidents meet, as they did in January of this year. This is an issue which is at the very center of the United States-China relationship.

So, we continue to work this problem. I have no magic bullet that is going to align our interest and China's interest entirely, with regard to North Korea. But, like so many other problems in the world, we have to keep working at it, chipping away, trying to advance the ball, if you will, because I am also of the view that it's very difficult to see an acceptable result to the challenges posed by North Korea without China's active participation.

The CHAIRMAN. Do you——

Sorry, did you want to add to that?

Dr. CAMPBELL. I would just add one thing to that, Senator, if I could. You had the opportunity to visit with President Hu Jintao when he visited Washington not long ago. In the intensive diplomacy surrounding his visit and the release of the United States-China joint statement, one of the central issues of our discussion was the developments on the Korean Peninsula.

And it's clear that the recent revelations associated with the alleged UEP program in North Korea have caused anxiety in Beijing. And they acknowledge that, for the first time, in our joint statement. It is the case that China takes very seriously the 2005 joint statement, whereby North Korea has made specific commitments about what it's prepared to do in the nuclear realm. And Chinese interlocutors view actions that North Korea has taken with regard to this program as being inconsistent with their declarations associated with the 2005 agreement.

The CHAIRMAN. Would you say that we have additional arrows in our quiver?

Ambassador BOSWORTH. Well, we always have, I think, in almost every situation, arrows in our quiver that we could employ. The question is: Do those contribute to bringing about a solution that is acceptable to us?

The CHAIRMAN. Well, if—I mean——

Ambassador BOSWORTH. But, I think—I don't mean to be——

The CHAIRMAN. No, but if you don't, then they're not usable. Maybe, I should——

Ambassador BOSWORTH. Well——

The CHAIRMAN [continuing]. Say "usable"——

[Laughter.]

Ambassador BOSWORTH. I think—and this is the way I kind of approach this issue of China and North Korea—that both of us have a major stake in demonstrating that working together with our other partners in the region, we can solve this problem or at least manage this problem over the longer term, because I think, in some sense, it is a litmus test to the ability of the United States and China to work together on broader issues.

The CHAIRMAN. To what do you attribute the increase of this volatility, active events between the North and the South, over the course of the last year or so?

Ambassador BOSWORTH. That's a very good question, and it's one that our intelligence community has worked at very assiduously. There is some belief that it is related to issues regarding succession in North Korea. There is some belief that it is related to jockeying among various factions in North Korea. I think it's also very important to look at the historical origins of these particular provocations as they arise.

I don't have an overall explanation for why these things have happened. I do think it is a useful reminder—an important reminder—of the extraordinary tension that exists along that border, along the DMZ, and of the importance of the United States and all of our other partners in trying to work to reduce that tension and manage the situation.

The CHAIRMAN. Last question, Secretary, if you don't mind. With respect to the North, this tension, do you believe that if we put the regime change/stability, whatever you want to call it—longevity—in other words, if the end product were that if they behave in XYZ ways, then we're not setting out to change the regime, that there's an open thing, and if China were to agree to that—is that the big, final enchilada for them? Is that the big deal that——

Ambassador BOSWORTH. Well, I think, clearly, for the North Koreans, regime continuity is the essential objective of everything that they do. We have indicated to them strongly, on a number of occasions over the last few years, that we do not regard regime change as the outcome of our policy. But, we do regard a change in regime behavior as necessary to any fundamental improvement in the overall relationship. We have, in the past, under various administrations in this country, held out the prospect of negative security assurances. We have repeatedly told them, particularly in the last 2 years, that regime change is not the objective of our policy. I told my interlocutors that when I visited North Korea in December 2009.

So, I think it may be that they don't believe us or that they don't fully trust us. But, I don't think they should be operating under the fear that somehow we are dedicated and determined to undermine the regime.

The CHAIRMAN. Senator Lugar.

Senator LUGAR. Thank you, Mr. Chairman.

As I mentioned in my opening statement, I asked the Congressional Research Service to evaluate the implementation of U.N. Security Council Resolution 1874, and they reported that implementation with regard to the sanctions has been uneven globally and, in cases, diminished over time. Now, in addition to that problem, there is the problem of the trading partners and the actual or potential proliferation of elements of the nuclear program to other countries.

I would like for your comment on the Congressional Research Service's finding about the uneven or even diminishing application of sanctions.

Ambassador BOSWORTH. Well——

Senator LUGAR [continuing]. And the sending out by the North Koreans, either for profit in the regime or personally, of elements of the nuclear program.

Ambassador BOSWORTH. Well, first of all, I would agree that implementation has been uneven. But, to improve implementation has been one of the fundamental goals of our multilateral diplomacy. And we have a number of people, who travel the world, in fact, talking to individual governments about the need to tighten sanctions against North Korea and to fully implement the sanctions resolutions of the U.N. Security Council.

Dr. CAMPBELL. Can I just—also, if I could, Senator, just to add to that. I think it would be fair to say that North Korea is probably the most heavily sanctioned country in the world. As Ambassador Bosworth has indicated, we have a fairly elaborate set of steps that we are taking in a variety of countries.

And I would point to a number of successes that perhaps do not get enough attention. In the last year, a number of states who had previously never been involved in, shall we say, interdicting or helping us with the transfer of illicit cargoes from North Korea to sites either in Asia or in the Middle East have assisted us in turning back shipments. We've also been able to target some specific entities that are involved in providing hard currency to elite groups around the leadership. And our evidence suggests that, in fact, many of these efforts do indeed bite and have created some difficulties, overall, for the leadership.

I think it'd be fair to say that there is more to be done and that this is an issue that we engage actively on, particularly with our friends, not just in Japan and South Korea, but also in China. As we speak right now, we have a senior team in China discussing these very matters.

Senator LUGAR. Well, there were some allegations, for example, that North Korean nuclear materials reached Syria at one point. I'm just curious—maybe these are only elements that our intelligence services are examining, but are there periodic reports, by the State Department or by somebody, as to how the sanctions are working? In other words, reports that detail, country by country, what the nature of the cooperation is. What have we caught? What got away? This sort of thing.

Ambassador BOSWORTH. Sure. No, we look at all those issues very carefully. And I think I can commit the administration—if you would like us to follow up in an executive session, and examine some of these specific cases, I think we would be very happy to do so. For reasons I know you will understand, some of these are a little too sensitive to discuss in an open hearing.

Senator LUGAR. I do understand that, but I wanted to raise the issue——

Ambassador BOSWORTH. Sure.

Senator LUGAR [continuing]. Because I think it's a critical one, not just in terms of our relations with North Korea, but in terms of difficulties elsewhere in the world, where some of this material may wind up.

Ambassador BOSWORTH. Without question. And I would say, for the record, that proliferation of nuclear materials and missile materials coming out of North Korea is one of our major concerns and is one of the major factors driving American policy in this regard.

Senator LUGAR. I'd like to inquire about North Korea's work with the Burmese military. There have been reports, from time to time, that we have tried to dissuade a North Korean ship from reaching a projective destination in Burma. But, what is the general consensus as to where that relationship is? And how does it affect the six-power talks or others in which Burma is not a part?

Dr. CAMPBELL. Thank you, Senator. I appreciate the question.

I think it would be fair to say that, in the past, most of North Korea's proliferation activities have affected the Middle East. But, in the recent period, they have increased substantially, we believe, the provision of certain conventional technologies—small arms and also some missile components—to Burma, in strict and clear violation of U.N. Security Council resolutions. We continue to monitor other allegations closely, associated with illicit activities between North Korea and Burma.

This is a subject of enormous concern. And we have worked closely with a number of countries in Southeast Asia to assist us in establishing a greater degree of confidence about illicit transfers, largely by ship, coming from North Korea.

This is one of those areas that Ambassador Bosworth has indicated that we'd be pleased to perhaps engage with you in private session. I will tell you, we've had some successes, but this is an enormously challenging problem. And, in fact, North Korea, in many of these areas, has demonstrated itself, that they are a determined proliferator. And, as Ambassador Bosworth has indicated, this is at the top of our list, in terms of our overall concerns.

Senator LUGAR. Well, I appreciate the sensitivity. Once again, perhaps this could be more thoroughly discussed in a classified session.

Let me, finally, ask: Recently, a South Korean lawmaker suggested the United States redeploy tactical nuclear weapons to South Korea as a deterrent to North Korea. What is the perspective of either of you on that suggestion?

Ambassador BOSWORTH. Well, I've seen those reports. Let me just say that our mission in South Korea is to deter any aggression by North Korea. And we are very confident that we have more than adequate tools at our disposal to accomplish that mission of deterrence.

Senator LUGAR. So, as a result of that, you——

Ambassador BOSWORTH. We have no—I mean, this is not an issue that is under active consideration.

Senator LUGAR. I thank you.

Thank you, Mr. Chairman.

The CHAIRMAN. Thank you, Senator Lugar.

Senator Risch.

Senator RISCH. Thank you, Senator Kerry.

Gentlemen, thank you for your service. Certainly, you've got one of the most difficult tasks of anybody in Foreign Service.

And, you know, I've read your opening statements and listened carefully. And I've been to South Korea and compared the two governments. Obviously, I've never been to North Korea. But, the one thing that, in my mind, makes this such a knotty problem is, you can't really understand what makes these people tick. You know, before you can resolve a problem, you've got to understand the problem. And I'm at a loss as to an explanation as to what motivates the North Korean regime. What is it that makes them feel good? What is it that makes them feel bad? Why do they do the things that they do?

I mean, you know, if they were an individual human being, they'd probably be committed because of their inconsistencies and what the psychiatrists call "inappropriate behavior." It's just—it's nonunderstandable. Can you try to shed some light on that for me?

Ambassador BOSWORTH. Well, I'm not sure that I can illuminate that whole question, but what I would say is that what I find useful in trying to understand North Korean behavior is to understand that everything that the North Korean Government does, domestically and internationally, is aimed at one goal, and that is perpetuation of the regime.

Senator RISCH. And I understand that. But, you know, that's not unique to North Korea. I mean, there's——

Ambassador BOSWORTH. No——

Senator RISCH [continuing]. There's many, many countries in the world—now, I agree it's—that is there, on steroids, but there's a lot of regimes in the world that are focused on——

Ambassador BOSWORTH. I think when you combine that singular goal with the existence of what is probably one of the most comprehensive police states in the history of the organized world, you can get some insight into how that place operates. But, it remains, as Churchill said about the Soviet Union in the 1940s, "an enigma wrapped in a mystery," or maybe it was the other way around. We don't know that much about how North Korea works, internally. We don't know that much about how decisions are made. And, in the end, we don't know that much about who makes them.

Senator RISCH. Well, I appreciate that. And again, you know, when you step back and you look at people who are in power or in charge, and you look at the way they treat their fellow human beings that are the same—their fellow countrymen—I mean, it is just—it's just staggering to try to get your arms around it and understand what—how they think. And—Mr. Campbell, you want to take a run at it?

Dr. CAMPBELL. Well, thank you, Senator. I would associate myself with the comments of Ambassador Bosworth.

I will say that it is among our most difficult intelligence challenges, to understand what goes on. And I would say that it's not simply the survival of the regime; I'd be more particular. It's the survival of the family, of Kim Jong-il and its very, very narrow group of people at the very, very top of the system.

And indeed, they have practiced internal brutality of a kind that we've seen in very few places globally. And the level of isolation that their population generally experiences is probably unmatched anywhere else in the world. And that is a very determined effort on the part of the leadership.

And I will tell you, one of the interesting tensions that exists, I think, between China and North Korea is that for years China has attempted to encourage the leadership to open up economically, to practice a form of, shall we say, authoritarian reform of the kind that the Soviet Union—that China practiced after Deng Xiaoping came to power. And I think they have been very discouraged by the fact that North Korea has essentially chosen not to follow that path. It is still an extraordinarily isolated country.

And I think that the general prism that Ambassador Bosworth laid out, which is to try to think about every step they take as part of a larger strategy to try to maintain and secure the leadership of Kim Jong-il and his chosen successor.

Senator RISCH. I understand the proposition that they want to stay in power and they do everything they can—that's their single objective. But, you know, really, what they do on these brinksmanship things doesn't really mesh with that, because, I mean, if you wanted to stay in power, what you'd want is to keep the seas calm and keep things the way they are. Instead, they go out and they sink a ship or they do an artillery attack on South Korea. Why would you do that if you truly did want to keep things just exactly as they were? I mean, it——

Ambassador BOSWORTH. Well——

Senator RISCH [continuing]. Just doesn't make sense.

Ambassador BOSWORTH [continuing]. They want to preserve the regime, but they also want the world's attention, because they need things from the outside world. And so, they do this—these provocations, both to demonstrate that they remain a force to be reckoned with—they do not want to be ignored—and they do them because they think, as the cycle advances, that our response will provide them benefits.

Senator RISCH. Thank you.

Again, gentlemen, thank you so much for your service. And I can tell you, I sincerely appreciate the difficult Rubik's Cube you're dealing with here.

Thank you.

Senator LUGAR [presiding]. Well, thank you, Senator Risch.

Senator Rubio.

Senator RUBIO. Thank you, Secretary and Ambassador.

I want to just kind of build on what Senator Risch was talking about, and then maybe focus more tightly on the nuclear ambitions of North Korea, which just takes so much of our attention and energy.

It sounds—I'm neither an expert on Korea or on Asia, but it sounds, from the testimony here today and what I read before being here today, and following all the things that have been written about the region leading up to this hearing here today, that clearly at the core of the nuclear ambitions of this country is survival, in essence. Most countries develop a nuclear capacity, (a) because, for example, India and Pakistan are largely focused on each other, and clearly the cold war is something we fully understand. From North Korea's perspective, it doesn't seem like they're in fear of a Japanese invasion or, quite frankly, an American one. This is, basically—as far as I can see, is an insurance policy. It is the—it is something that they—their ability to have a nuclear program makes them, not just a force to be reckoned with in the region, because of the damage they can do, but, quite frankly, gives them some level of security and fear that there's limits on what the United States or any other actor can do against North Korea's interests, because of their capacity to react with a nuclear weapon. Is that a—I mean, is that basically a accurate description of the purpose——

Ambassador BOSWORTH. Well, let me——

Senator RUBIO [continuing]. Of the nuclear program?

Ambassador BOSWORTH. Let me try to respond to it, then maybe Kurt Campbell will have something to add.

I think they view a nuclear weapons program as the ultimate deterrent. This is a country that has, for 60 years or more, lived in, sort of, day-to-day fear of being invaded or being attacked from the outside. Rightly or wrongly—they may exaggerate that, but, rightly or wrongly, that's what they believe. So, for them, a stockpile of nuclear weapons constitutes the ultimate deterrent. And they consider it essential to their regime's survival.

Senator RUBIO. If I could just touch upon that. They don't actually even have to have the weapons, right? They just have to show the capacity to build them and to deliver it, if they ever wanted to.

Ambassador BOSWORTH. I think that's correct.

Senator RUBIO. What I'm trying to get at is, is that we spend all this time and energy trying to convince ourselves that we're going to be able to ever talk them out of the program. It sounds to me that, in essence, the program is the regime. It is the core and essence of its existence and ability to survive. I mean, they're certainly not going to stay in power because they're doing a good job managing the economy. They're not going to stay in power because they do a good job of distributing justice. The one thing that keeps them in power is the ability to crack down on internal dissent and the ability to repel foreign intervention in their affairs, because of this nuclear program. And so, it seems to me like this idea, that we're going to somehow be able to pressure and/or convince them to abandon this program—the price of pressuring them seems like it's extraordinarily high, given the central importance that this has on their regime; I mean, on its very survival.

Ambassador BOSWORTH. I don't think anyone in the administration—I certainly do not underestimate the difficulty of negotiating on the path that we are on, toward a comprehensive and irreversible, verifiable end to North Korea's nuclear weapons program. I have some belief that, in the longer term, as we pursue this program, if we can pursue this policy effectively, that a mix of incentives and disincentives can be found which will make North Korea more willing to contemplate giving up the program. In the meantime, along the way, there are important things that I think we can try to achieve relating to the question of proliferation, relating to their production of fissile material, both from their plutonium program and from their uranium enrichment program.

So, I think simply to say now, "Well, we'll never convince them to give up these weapons," is probably an error, because, as we pursue the ultimate goal—and I think, given our global nonproliferation policy, we must pursue that ultimate goal—but, as we pursue it, I think other things become achievable and, in the end, we may actually get "yes" for an answer. But, if we don't try, we're certainly not going to get "yes" for an answer.

Ambassador BOSWORTH. Yes.

Senator RUBIO. But—and I'm not suggesting that we should—but, the question, I guess, is there's two separate topics; one is proliferation. And clearly, that's the one that I do believe we could have some influence over. But, what I'm trying to really kind of arrive at an answer—is this mix of incentives versus disincentives of even having a program or having the capacity to have a program. It's hard for me to envision what that mix of disincentives that would lead to them abandoning the program is.

Dr. CAMPBELL. Can I, Senator, just take one other shot at that? I like very much the way Ambassador Bosworth laid this out. But, I will say, it was only a few years ago that a number of people, who, for instance, were looking at some of the developments in Libya, thought that it would be impossible to create any kind of program whereby a very secretive but determined program that Gaddafi was undertaking in the nuclear realm would be stopped. But, through purposeful diplomacy in the Bush administration, we achieved that. And just imagine the circumstances today in Libya if there was a nuclear dimension. There'd be—it's tremendously dangerous now, but it would be horrifically so if there was an added nuclear dimension.

So, I think that the diplomacy aimed at this is a worthy goal, overall. And I think that you have to take it in pieces. And one of the most important elements here is on the matter of proliferation, as Ambassador Bosworth indicated.

I will also say that, you know, North Korea is one of the most militarized states in the world. And so, it not only has the nuclear program that we have been discussing, but it has one of the largest conventional forces, including artillery, that is arrayed just above the DMZ within easy, and unfortunately, ready striking distance of one of the largest cities in the world: Seoul. And so, it has other means at its disposal to be able to provide some form of deterrent.

I think the truth is that the risks, particularly on the proliferation side, are so great, and the concerns associated with other elements that are transpiring inside the country suggest that this sort of determined approach to diplomacy is the right course for the United States.

Senator RUBIO. And I guess what I'm really trying to get at—and I think it's going to be an ongoing dialogue—is, I'm trying to picture, in my head, what that would look like. What set of conditions or disincentives or incentives, what kind of package of those would it take to tilt the scales for a regime of this nature? And these are—this is not just a pragmatic—this is not some sort of pragmatic government that's looking to build its economy and grow its country. Above everything else, according to the testimony here today and everything we've seen, what they're really interested in is owning this country for as long as they can, and staying in power, as a family. I'm just trying to figure out what set of incentives/disincentives it would take to tilt that scale toward abandonment of this capacity and this program. Obviously, sitting here, it's not a—you know, the ideal setting to, kind of, have a——

Ambassador BOSWORTH. Right.

Senator RUBIO [continuing]. Conversation about that—but how that's developed, and, in our mind, whether that's even realistic. And I think we have a similar conversation going on with regards to Iran and other parts of the world. But, this one's even more problematic, because we know so little about its decisionmaking process and things of that nature.

I don't know if I have time, Chairman, to ask a real quick question, because I know I'm a little bit——

Senator LUGAR. Go ahead.

Senator RUBIO. Just, I wanted to talk briefly about the humanitarian aid. Again, this is an issue of first impression, to me, having—this is my second meeting on this committee. I'm interested in the food program in the past. And how problematic has it been, in terms of seeing those resources diverted to elites or the military?

Ambassador BOSWORTH. Well, as I indicated earlier, Senator, one of the conditions that we have imposed—I think, successfully, for the most part—on our provision of food aid, has been a very careful process of monitoring. Now, I wouldn't want to exaggerate that. We don't have an outside monitor following every bag of grain that is put into the country. But, we agree with the North Koreans, in advance, on the recipients of the USAID, which includes, of course, children, older people, et cetera. And then, through frequent inspection, we have been able to verify—quite effectively, we think—that the aid has gone to the recipients for whom it was intended.

Now, we negotiated this monitoring arrangement back in 2007, I believe—2007/2008. In 2009, the North Koreans threw out our food assistance team—some people believe, because they became concerned that having Korean-speaking outsiders—and many of the United States team were Korean speakers—was not in their long-term interest, so they threw them out, which is another indication that perhaps they were quite effective.

But, as we indicated in our respective testimonies, we are currently assessing need. We have some other things that we need to do in response to North Korea's request for renewed food aid. And then we will talk to the North Koreans about a monitoring system, which, at its minimum, would be as effective as the one that we had there last time.

Dr. CAMPBELL. Can I just add to that, Senator?

Just, as part of this, we would also be in very close coordination with our colleagues on Capitol Hill, who have a very keen interest in this and have provided very useful context for how to think about this overall program.

I just want to underscore that no decisions have been made. We are still in the study phase. And we are taking this matter very seriously. And we're in close coordination with our South Korean colleagues, as well.

I will say, one of the key conditions that I find most powerful is that the packaging—and I've seen them myself and would love to send one up to your office—makes very clear to the recipients that this food assistance comes from the United States, from the people of the United States. And so, it's very clear, impossible to disguise, that when this food is distributed, it is well understood that it comes from the benevolence of United States people.

The CHAIRMAN [presiding]. Senator, thank you.

Just a couple of quick questions.

What's the impact of the uranium enrichment program disclosure, in terms of our overall interests there?

Ambassador BOSWORTH. Well, first of all, this did not come as a complete surprise to us. We have long—as you know, Mr. Chairman—long suspected that North Korea was pursuing a program of uranium enrichment. They then, of course, as we all know, showed this facility to a group of visiting Americans, including one of our more prominent nuclear scientists. We know that the centrifuges are there. We cannot verify that they are operating. And we cannot verify that they've had any production of enriched uranium.

But, I would say, without question, two things. One, this means that, assuming we do get back to the table with them, that is very much going to be the No. 1 issue on our list of concerns and things that we have to talk about. The other is that a viable uranium enrichment program does present a complication to our efforts to negotiate a denuclearization agreement with the North Koreans, no question about it. Verification becomes an even more difficult question. And obviously, these are subjects that we're going to have to get at with them.

The CHAIRMAN. To what degree do South Korean interests and/or politics constrain what we might or might not want to do at this point?

Ambassador BOSWORTH. On the matter of uranium enrichment?

The CHAIRMAN. No, on the matter of——

Ambassador BOSWORTH. Or just in general?

The CHAIRMAN [continuing]. In general, engagement/talks. Bilateral.

Ambassador BOSWORTH. Well, I don't think they constrain our reaction and our ability to act. We have said, to both the South Koreans and, more importantly, to the North Koreans, that, from our point of view, an improvement in South/North relations, particularly after the blatant provocations of the last year, is a necessary step before we can resume a more multilaterally oriented negotiating process or dialogue. And we saw, early last month, a tentative step forward in that regard, on the part of the North and South Korean militaries. We are optimistic—or hopeful, at least— that that step will be followed by others. We've made it very clear to North Korea and to China that South Korea is the aggrieved party in this instance, and, as our ally, we're standing with them. And we want to see some change and improvement in North Korean attitude on key points of interest to South Korea.

Dr. CAMPBELL. Let me just add to that, if I could, Senator, very quickly.

I think it's very important for Americans to understand the tremendous forbearance and, frankly, the courage that the South Korean, particularly President Lee Myung-bak, have demonstrated in the face of repeated outrageous provocations. And the fact that they have been calm and not responded in a retaliatory way is a tremendous testament to their leadership.

And I would probably even go further than what Ambassador Bosworth has said, although I agree with everything he has said, that very few countries in the world have demonstrated how much they are prepared to work with the United States, not just on the Peninsula, but globally. South Korea's foreign assistance, their commitment to Afghanistan, to what we're doing globally, is remarkable. They are emerging as a key player on the international stage. They have played an important role in the G20. I think this emerging partnership between the United States and South Korea in this new phase is one of the most important success stories of Northeast Asia.

So, I would say, overall, our diplomacy and our approaches are reinforcing. And I think one of the reasons why South Korea was able to respond so carefully to these provocations was indeed the strength and confidence they had of the relationship with the United States.

The CHAIRMAN. What could either of you share with us about Japan's back-channel efforts with this—in this regard, over the course of the last year?

Ambassador BOSWORTH. Let me first talk about the front-channel efforts. One of the things that's been most important over the course of the last year has been the extent to which this new Japanese Government is prepared to work constructively with South Korea. I think, as you know, we have some long memories in Asia. There have been some historical differences and challenges between Japan and South Korea. What we have seen has been a forward-looking and progressive effort by Japan to support South Korea in the face of these provocations.

Last December, Secretary Clinton hosted, for the first time, a ministerial-level trilateral, with her colleagues from Japan and South Korea, in which all three countries worked very closely together to demonstrate cooperation with respect to North Korea.

I think Japan is prepared to be extraordinarily supportive within the context of the six-party framework. And they have been very transparent in all their activities in Northeast Asia, with both South Korea and the United States.

The CHAIRMAN. Ambassador, I mentioned, a little while ago, you'd made seven trips to Beijing. But, it's my understanding you've only made one to Pyongyang. Have we——

Ambassador BOSWORTH. That is correct.

The CHAIRMAN. Have we kind of isolated ourselves, here?

Ambassador BOSWORTH. No; I don't believe so. You know, we've made it clear, I'm prepared to go to——

The CHAIRMAN. What's the seven-to-one ratio? Why wouldn't you pop over——

Ambassador BOSWORTH. It's an even larger ratio with regard to my trips to South Korea, because I think, at this stage in our efforts to deal with this set of problems, we find that it's, above all, first, important to coordinate our efforts with our partners in the six-party process.

The CHAIRMAN. Somebody—I mean, is there a resistance, here, to saying, "Let's get back to the table"?

Ambassador BOSWORTH. No, I think we are very open to getting back to the table, provided, as I indicated earlier, that's done under the right set of circumstances and in the right framework.

The CHAIRMAN. Who's going to figure that out?

Ambassador BOSWORTH. Well, we're all, collectively, trying to figure that out. And I——

The CHAIRMAN. Do you have to talk to them to figure it out?

Ambassador BOSWORTH. Well, we are not without ways of communicating with them. And we do communicate with them. But, I think, ultimately, we may have to have further conversations with them, bilaterally, in order to figure out how to move forward multilaterally.

The CHAIRMAN. Senator Lugar, do you have any additional——

Senator LUGAR. One short question, sort of referring back to my mention of the 8,000 Americans from the Korean war that are not accounted for. First of all, is there any information on this matter coming from the North Koreans? And, second, apparently there has been some search, in Chinese military archives, as to who might have been taken into China from North Korea during that conflict, and perhaps some cooperation with the Chinese. On either front, do you have information or an idea of whether this is being pursued?

Dr. CAMPBELL. Thank you, Senator Lugar.

First of all, let me just underscore that we, in the U.S. Government, have had a consistent policy that the recovery of remains, the identification of Missing in Action, remains an extraordinarily high priority for our activities. And we've demonstrated that in Southeast Asia in other conflicts, and also on the Korean Peninsula.

I think it would be fair to say that we view the program in North Korea as a critical humanitarian effort. I think the North Koreans view it largely as an opportunity to raise hard currency. We are prepared, under the right circumstances, to resume this overall effort.

I think, particularly when it relates to the interactions that we've had with China over the course of many years associated with the North Korean—excuse me, with the Korean war—let me take that question for the record, and I will get back to you directly with where this specifically stands. I remember it very closely from my time working in the Department of Defense, but I'm not sure where it stands currently. And I will get back to you directly.

[EDITOR'S NOTE.—the information requested above was not available when this hearing went to press.]

Senator LUGAR. I would thank you for that report.

Thank you, sir.

The CHAIRMAN. Senator Rubio, do you have any questions for——

Senator RUBIO. Just one more, kind of, question/observation, to either one of you, and maybe both. You know, I've read in a couple of places some—whether it's opposition folks outside of North Korea or what have you—one of the arguments that has been made is that, clearly, in a country that's struggling with poverty and a lot of suffering, you have a government willing to spend between 15 and 25 percent of its gross domestic product on the military, particularly a very expensive nuclear program, a nuclear ambition. And the argument is that the—in a country that's willing to do that, that this food assistance is basically going to be taken and used to feed the elites and the military, and that, in essence—I've read somewhere, and I'm not saying I agree with this—but that food program, in many respects, relieves the pressure on the North Korean Government to divert funds away from the nuclear program and divert it toward—and place it to where it should be, which is feeding and caring for its people. Do you have thought—and you probably have read some of those statements that have been made by some—and do you have any thoughts on that, in general?

Ambassador BOSWORTH. My general thoughts on that, Senator, would be that it's, I think, indicative of the nature of that regime that they're prepared to do this. My second observation would be that, in my experience, the last group of people in North Korea who will not have food are the military. So, if we provide food, and if we can monitor it carefully and we know that it's going to children, institutional needs, I think it's the right thing to do.

Senator RUBIO. I think that the argument that some have made—and not that I'm making it today, but the argument that some have made is that, the fact that we—that, to the extent that food does get to people in North Korea—and it's a very calloused approach, I understand—but someone have made the argument that, to the extent that food and goods does gets to people, what it does is, it takes pressure off the regime to have to take that money away from its nuclear program and instead divert it to its people, where it should be in the first place.

Dr. CAMPBELL. Can I say, Senator, I don't think—that would be the kind of calculus that a Western government that heeds the needs of its people would perhaps take into account—I don't think the North Korean leadership believes in these kinds of tradeoffs. I think they are committed to these programs that you have described. And they have demonstrated, historically, that they are prepared to allow enormous suffering. Very substantial component of its population suffered through starvation in parts of the 1990s. And so, the choice really, here, is whether these people are allowed to starve. And that's, frankly, a humanitarian issue, really not a one of political discourse.

Ambassador BOSWORTH. North Korea's national strategy continues to be, as it has been for several years, something called a military-first strategy. And they allocate resources accordingly.

Senator RUBIO. It sounds like the testimony, basically, is that they're willing to let their people starve. In essence, they don't respond to that kind of pressure; it's not part of their decisionmaking matrix.

My last question. And again, because this is kind of an issue of first impression to me. Unification and—as a realistic goal in the long term or midterm, you know, what—is there a national identity that crosses from North to South? And I—No. 2, my first impression on this—and you may be able to elaborate more on it—is that a unification of North and South Korea, from a pragmatic standpoint, looks like it would be even more difficult than an East and West Germany unification was, for example, just given the dramatic differences between the two economies. But, what is the status of that? How realistic is that? How much is that discussed? How much is that desired?

Ambassador BOSWORTH. Well, I think most South Koreans would agree that the cost of reunifying the Korean Peninsula is going to be enormous. That does not mean, however, that they do not hold this, still, as a strongly desired national objective. But, the sense of Koreanness between South and North remains very deep, even though, over the last several decades, the two countries have gone in such different directions that it is very difficult to, sort of, automatically see the way in which that will happen.

I think, quite clearly, it's not going to happen on the basis of the North Korean political economic model. It is—and the South Korean political economic model would be a more feasible route. But, that presumes all sorts of things happening, over which we have very little way to forecast right now.

Dr. CAMPBELL. Can I just——

Senator RUBIO. Is there——

Dr. CAMPBELL. Can I just——

Senator RUBIO. I'm sorry.

Dr. CAMPBELL. Sorry, Senator. I didn't mean to—I would say the—what I find interesting, in interacting with Korean friends, is I think they have both a bond—a deep, historical, cultural bond—but it coexists with a deep alienation. So, I think what's challenging about the Korean Peninsula is that, for most, particularly South Korean citizens, they feel both—both an attraction, a deep recognition of historical kinship, and cultural sameness, but also a deep alienation. And spanning that gap will be enormously challenging in the future.

Senator RUBIO. My last question.

What is the Chinese view—is there an official Chinese view on unification—officially, unofficially—your impressions on how they would view that. Particularly since I think we would all agree that any reunification would look more like South Korea than North Korea, for obvious reasons.

Ambassador BOSWORTH. My impression is that, from Beijing, the current organization on the Korean Peninsula looks about as good as they would—they could imagine.

Senator RUBIO. In essence, you think they like it just the way it is.

Ambassador BOSWORTH. Yes. Not all aspects of it just the way it is, but Korean reunification is not one of the major objectives of the Chinese Government.

Senator RUBIO. So, suffice it to say that a unified Korea that looks like South Korea and has the kind of close relationship with the United States that South Korea now has is not high on their wish list.

Ambassador BOSWORTH. I would put it that way, yes.

The CHAIRMAN. Thank you.

Thank you, folks.

Mr. Secretary and Mr. Ambassador, thanks a lot for being here.

We're going to leave the record open for a week. We had some colleagues who wanted to be here, who couldn't be here. So, if you don't mind, we'll try not to burden you, but we do want to make sure the record is complete.

If I could ask for the second panel to come up while this panel is departing: L. Gordon Flake, executive director of Mansfield Foundation; Marcus Noland, Peterson Institute for International Economics; and Robert Carlin, Center for International Security and Cooperation, Stanford.

And if—I'd ask, Mr. Carlin, if you would lead off; Director Noland, if you'd go second; and, Mr. Flake, if you'd wrap up.

Thank you.

Can we keep order, please, in the hearing. I want to keep moving forward.

Mr. Carlin.

## STATEMENT OF ROBERT CARLIN, CENTER FOR INTERNATIONAL SECURITY AND COOPERATION, STANFORD UNIVERSITY, STANFORD, CA

Mr. CARLIN. Thank you, sir. It's a pleasure and an honor to be here.

Once upon a time, we learned three useful lessons dealing with North Korea: It was possible to advance key U.S. interests through talks with them. In those talks, our negotiators could break down complex problems into component parts, and then deal with those parts in logical order. And finally, contrary to the common wisdom, if an agreement was well conceived, constructed, and implemented, the North Koreans would abide by the core of it, as long as we did. We knew, of course, that they'd game the process and hedge their bets.

These are not theoretical lessons; they come from hard experience. But, we did a bad job explaining this to the Congress and to the American people. And so, everything that we learned and accomplished was buried under a mountain of myth. Instead, today the phrase, "We won't buy the same horse twice," is considered wisdom. Though it is based on the mistaken belief that negotiating with the DPRK is simple flimflammery.

Some in Washington may remember, in the early 1990s, that discussions on North Korea policy had, as part of the agenda, preparing for something that was called a "soft landing." The goal was to prevent a calamity of the destabilizing situation that would result from a collapse of the North.

This concept of a soft landing had a number of advantages for us. Notably, it didn't handcuff us to fixed goals. It allowed us room to maneuver, to protect and pursue our national interests, as the situation warranted. Then, as now, many people did not see the point in talking to the North Koreans, because they considered our problems in Korea primarily military. But, the North's development of a nuclear program in the late 1980s meant that the issue for us had become as much diplomatic as military. And it still is.

It was clear that the North Koreans wanted to talk. But, why? We developed a fairly good understanding, over hundreds and hundreds of hours, as we listened to them. But, then abruptly in 2001, the talking stopped, and apparently so did the listening. And, not incidentally, all of our previous gains were cast overboard. As a result, the situation today is much more difficult. Our leverage is smaller, not greater. And our room for maneuver has become even more curtailed.

If there was a chance, 10 years ago, of stopping the North from building a small nuclear arsenal, the gain has now changed, and it has not changed in our favor.

I worked under seven U.S. Presidents. I don't think our problem dealing with the North is confined to one administration or one party. I think, in the deepest sense, the problems reflect a very curious national inability to fathom how states like North Korea work and how they see the world.

Our difficulties are compounded by the fact that our public discourse in this country about North Korea has for too long been condescending and irrelevant. The general impression in the United States is that North Koreans live in a blasted moonscape. And any observer contradicting that image, even purely as a matter of fact, becomes suspect.

As we heard earlier, the word has gone out that we aim to force the North to change its unacceptable behavior. If that is our goal, I'm afraid that the climb is going to be steeper than we imagine, because the North Koreans believe, if they behave simply on our say-so, they will become part of the woodwork of the great powers.

We constantly hear that the North Koreans inhabit the most isolated country on Earth. Yet, in some ways, we are more isolated from them than they are from the rest of the world. DPRK officials travel. They tune in outside radio. And they read outside books and newspapers detailing our politics and our society. By contrast, at least at the official level, we remain pristine. We don't go there. We rarely let them come here. And overall, we seem to keep contact as limited as we can.

The result? Well, to substitute for knowledge and experience, we have developed a fog of myths about North Korea. And amidst this fog, the North Koreans have learned to maneuver like Drake's small ships among the galleons of the Spanish Armada.

Ultimately, progress on the North Korean issue depends not on the pressures we bring to bear, but on how well we understand the regime. If we don't grasp that North Koreans believe they have legitimate national interests, then we fall into the trap of thinking we can force them, sweet-talk them, or bribe them into doing as we want. Diplomacy worked with North Korea when it's searched for those places where interests overlap. But, when we signal the North Koreans that there is no place for them in our vision of the future, we undermine the basis for serious discussion of circumstances in which we might, for now, coexist.

Do, in fact, such areas of overlapping interests still exist? It's hard to imagine getting at an answer if we don't actually sit down and explore the landscape.

Thank you.

[The prepared statement of Mr. Carlin follows:]

### Prepared Statement of Robert Carlin

Once upon a time, not so long ago, we learned three valuable lessons about dealing with North Korea.

First, it is indeed possible to advance U.S. national security interests through negotiations with Pyongyang. We even found that we had considerable leverage with the North Koreans if we did more than merely paint pictures for them of a sweet and fanciful future.

Second, in talks with the North it is possible to break down complex, seemingly insurmountable problems into component parts and then focus on the parts in a logical order, so that successfully dealing with the first (usually the easiest) boosts the chances of dealing with subsequent, more difficult items.

Third, contrary to the common wisdom, if an agreement is thoughtfully constructed and implemented, the North Koreans will abide by the core of it as long as we do. It should not be a surprise to discover, however that they are likely to game the process, exploiting ambiguities and hedging their bets.

These are not theoretical classroom lessons or the fruit of idle speculation. They come from real experience over many years.

Yet we did a poor job of explaining this experience to the Congress and to the American people. As a result, what we learned, as well as what we accomplished, was buried under a mountain of myth, where it has remained for many years.

Today, the catch phrase "we won't buy the same horse twice" is taken as wisdom in dealing with the challenges posed by North Korea. Unfortunately, it is based on the mistaken but all too easily accepted belief that negotiating with the DPRK is an exercise in flimflammery.

Twinned with that is an assumption, fervently held by many who should know better, that we have, or can garner, enough power to dictate outcomes to the North Koreans. And if they don't do as we insist, the thinking goes, we can wait until they collapse or the Chinese make them come around.

There may be a few still in Washington who remember that in the early 1990s, discussion about North Korea policy centered around the idea of preparing for a "soft landing"—that is, preventing the very scenario that takes up so much nervous energy in various capitals these days, a calamitous and highly destabilizing collapse of North Korea. The concept of a soft landing had a number of advantages as a core policy precept. Notably, it did not handcuff us to fixed and unachievable goals. Instead, it provided necessary maneuver room to pursue our national interests in dealing with the North as the situation warranted. What it did not allow or envision was sitting and waiting while another country shaped the future of Northeast Asia.

I am not attempting to describe a golden era of a lost age. For one thing, in those days, we still had much to learn about dealing with North Korea, at that point not having engaged the North except in the Military Armistice Commission talks at

Panmunjom. In fact, then as now many people didn't see the point in even talking to the North Koreans. Our problem on the peninsula was still seen as largely military.

A number of changes in the late 1980s, however, drove home that sending an aircraft carrier to cow the North was no longer a sufficient response. Inter-Korean dialogue and the North's development of a nuclear program meant that the issues for Washington had multiplied and that the challenges presented by the North had become as much diplomatic as military.

It was clear to us that the North Koreans wanted to talk—but why? We developed a pretty good idea 10 years ago as we listened to what they said and observed their reactions over hundreds and hundreds of hours of formal and informal contacts. Nor did we merely listen. We explained, we educated, and on occasion, we pounded the table.

But then, abruptly in 2001, we stopped talking and, apparently, stopped listening. As a result, we have lost a decade in which to deal with the situation on the Korean Peninsula. Not only that, in the bargain we tossed overboard all that we had previously gained. As a result, the situation we face today is much more difficult, our leverage is smaller not greater, and our room for maneuver is even more curtailed. If there was a chance 10 years ago that we might have stopped the North from conducting nuclear tests and building a small nuclear arsenal—and I believe we did have a good chance—the game has now changed, and not in our favor.

Let me be clear. Our problems dealing with North Korea are not confined to one administration or one party. In the deepest sense, they reflect our national inability, intellectually and emotionally, to understand how states like North Korea work. We fall into overly simplistic thinking. We trap ourselves into seeing only two dimensional figures. Our difficulties are compounded by the fact that public discourse about the North in the United States has long been crippled, condescending, irrelevant, and, like heartburn, episodic. There is a general impression in the United States that North Koreans live in a blasted landscape similar to the moon, and that all but a privileged few are hollow-eyed and slack-jawed. Any observer contradicting that image, even purely as a matter of fact, becomes suspect.

The word has gone out that we and our allies aim to force the North to change its "unacceptable behavior." We will not negotiate until the North creates the "conditions" for negotiations. If that is our goal, the climb is steeper than we imagine. Years ago, the North Koreans were taught, and the lesson has since been endlessly reinforced, that the world rarely rewards them for good behavior, because whatever they do is never deemed good enough. If they "behave," many North Koreans have become convinced that they will become part of the great power woodwork, something to be ignored and scuffed by the furniture on the way out.

It is widely and confidently stated that North Koreans inhabit the most isolated country on earth. How one would measure such a thing I have no idea, but assuming it approaches the truth, then it must also be true that we are isolated from them. Isolation, after all, is a two-way street.

Yet, in fact, we are more isolated from the North Koreans than they are from the rest of the world. Though the numbers are small in comparison to what are now world standards, DPRK delegations are constantly traveling abroad. DPRK officials tune in outside radio and television, read outside books and newspapers detailing our politics and society. By contrast, at the official level, we keep ourselves largely pristine, don't go there, rarely let them come here, and overall keep contact as limited as we can on the grounds that exposing them to our thinking and our society, our culture and our values is a benefit, a present, a gift. No visas for the DPRK State Orchestra because . . . well, because. The result? The North Koreans reap tactical benefit from our ignorance, while we develop as a substitute for knowledge a fog of myths about them. And through this fog the North Koreans have learned to maneuver pretty well, like Drake's small ships among the galleons of the Spanish armada.

Now that Pluto is no longer a planet, some people seem to think it has been replaced by North Korea in the universe of strange, cold, and distant places. As it happens, we could define Pluto out of existence. We cannot do the same with North Korea, even if at times our fondest hope is to hold our breath until the country goes away.

Ultimately, progress toward our goals in dealing with North Korea depends not so much on the weight of the force we bring to bear—sanctions, U.N. resolutions—but on how well we understand the North Korean regime and its views of domestic and foreign policy challenges. If we fail to grasp that North Koreans believe they have their own national interests, then we fall into the trap of thinking we can force them, sweet talk them, or bribe them into doing what we want.

To return to my first point, diplomacy has proven it can work with North Korea if it seeks to discover those places where interests overlap. To the extent that we signal to the North Koreans that we don't see a place for them in our vision of the future of the region, we undermine the basis for realistic discussion of the circumstances in which we might coexist. Do, in fact, such areas of overlapping interests still exist? It is hard to imagine getting at an answer if we don't actually sit down and explore the landscape. Insisting that the North Koreans must first demonstrate a strategic decision to accept our outcome is a sure way of going nowhere fast.

We don't have to know everything about the North to know enough to operate intelligently and effectively in our dealings with them. Here are five interrelated subjects on which a lot of homework remains to be done.

*The threat.* Compared to where we used to be in our perception of the North Korean military threat, I think we are now on firmer ground, certainly more realistic. I applaud the careful assessment in DNI Clapper's testimony earlier this month, as well as recent comments on this subject by General Sharp, the Commander of U.S. Forces Korea. North Korea is largely in deterrent-defensive mode—militarily, diplomatically, and in every other way. That, indeed, has been the case for quite a while, and to the extent we can factor that into our calculations and our actions, I believe it more likely we can make progress in dealing with the North. At the same time, and this is crucial, we should not fool ourselves into thinking that we have the North in a box. They have teeth, and as we have seen, they will use them if they feel threatened or toyed with.

*The economy.* Certainly within the memory of many people in North Korea, there was a time when the North was far ahead of China economically and was, to some extent, seen by parts of the Third World as a beacon of development. We tend to look at the North and see a country hopelessly backward; they see themselves as capable and modern thinking but down on their luck. They make occasional runs at fixing things. Whether they can actually sustain economic revitalization policies long enough to show results, I do not know. If history is a guide, they seem unlikely to get very far on that path without significant changes in how they formulate and apply such policies. Nevertheless, they know very well their economy is not doing well, and they are constantly looking for ways to do better. Again, taking this into account in our own approach can pay dividends. We're not talking here about "bribes" or a "buyout," but rather using the North's own momentum and goals in a way the helps us achieve our own.

*The succession.* At this point, there is no question that Kim Jong-il's youngest son is being groomed and, more than that, moved into position as the successor. Chinese visitors have met him several times. I trust that we have asked them for their impressions of him. Given how grossly inaccurate early assessments by many outside observers were of Kim Jong-il, I would urge caution in accepting most of what appears in the press (or even official reporting) about the son's personality or potential. In the absence of very good information to the contrary, I wouldn't operate on the assumption that the succession will fall apart, especially if it has several more years to take root. It was an article of faith of many analysts and governments in 1994 when Kim Jong-il took over from Kim Il-sung that he wouldn't last a year. Nearly 17 years later, one hopes they have learned from their mistakes.

*The "collapse."* Anything is possible once the dam breaks in a society that has for years been under extremely tight political and social constraints, but I wouldn't put my money on the likelihood of near-term North Korean collapse. Yes, of course it makes sense to think about that possibility and to develop scenarios for dealing with such a contingency. In my view, however, it does not make sense to base a policy on the assumption that a collapse will happen soon—that is, in the next 2-3 years. Even those in South Korea normally anxious to portray the North Korean regime as fraying at the edges do not want to lean too far forward at this moment in predicting the likelihood that the uprising contagion from the Middle East will reach North Korea. One thing that ought to be of concern, if we are to look at scenarios, is the possibility that if and when serious social and political unrest ever arrives in the North, it will quickly descend into violence that could make Libya look like a tea party, dragging outsiders into a prolonged, bloody struggle for power.

*The role of China.* One can get very cogent advice from any number of China experts. All I can say is that having watched Sino-North Korean relations for 30 years, my feeling is that many China experts tend to miss the point that Beijing views North Korea differently than how it views the rest of the world. Consequently, Beijing's policies toward the North often do not track with its broader foreign policy. Sino-Korean relations have had numerous ups and downs over the years. They are very warm right now, perhaps the closest they have ever been. They are unlikely to stay good forever, and we should not treat North Korea as if it is (nor should we want it to be) in China's pocket. But for several years to come, unless, South Korea or the United States do something to provide the North with an alternate future, the Chinese shadow over North Korea will grow more pronounced. Even if that translates into increased Chinese leverage over the North (which I tend to doubt), it doesn't mean we can breathe a sigh of relief.

North Korea obviously isn't the jewel in the crown in Northeast Asia, but how the Korean issue is handled will probably be a decisive factor influencing the region for decades to come. The basic problem we face on the Peninsula today is a hangover from the first half of the 20th century. It is, or ought to be, a constant reminder of policy missteps made many years ago by all sides.

I'd hope we would spare a little time and effort to ensure we don't make similar mistakes again. As much as fires in the rest of the world and issues at home loom large, there is no reason for us, through inattention or ignorance, to sow the seeds of problems that could bedevil East Asia for a long time to come.

Senator LUGAR [presiding]. Mr. Flake, would you please proceed.

### STATEMENT OF L. GORDON FLAKE, EXECUTIVE DIRECTOR, THE MANSFIELD FOUNDATION, WASHINGTON, DC

Mr. FLAKE. Thank you, Senator Lugar. It's my honor to be here, as well.

First, let me extend my compliments on the particular focus of this hearing. Rather than another kind of broad effort to understand the entirety of the North Korean conundrum, I think this focus on breaking out of the cycle of provocations is extremely useful, particularly given the fact that there has been a marked shift, over the last several years, that warrants the attention of our government and this committee in particular.

I would start by talking a little bit about where we stand. The previous panel identified several specific recent North Korean provocations which have been the cause for our attention. But, I think if you step back and look at the last 2 years alone in a broader context, there's a very disturbing trend.

For example: In early 2009, you had a North Korean long-range missile test and a North Korean nuclear test, both of which resulted in a very concerted response from the United Nations Security Council. If North Korea goes that route again, it's a pretty well-known and well-traveled road through which the international community will respond.

Following that, there were notable inter-Korean incidents, including the killing of a South Korean tourist in the Diamond Mountain tourist zone; and in November 2009, what the South Koreans call the Battle of Daecheong, another ship-to-ship incident on the West Sea. In both of these cases the likely South Korean response now is quite clear. And so, in some respects, the door on those types of provocations are closed, as well.

Of course, the events of last year are very well known. Without the option to confront South Korea ship-to-ship, the North Koreans proceeded to sink, in the dead of night, a South Korean Corvette, the *Cheonan*. We have now spent 6 or 7 months developing very strong antisubmarine warfare capabilities between the United States and South Korea. So, again, in some respects, that option is foreclosed to North Korea.

And yet, the fallacy remains that we are somehow deterring North Korea when recent events would indicate that they're just moving on to the next provocation. In this context, something that nobody expected came completely out of the blue, the shelling of

Yeonpyeong Island and the dramatic declarations of the week prior about North Korea's uranium enrichment program. Again events which shocked the world and put us in the situation where we are today.

While recognizing that there has, at the same time, been a bit of a pendulum-swing between North Korean's inducements/offers for talks, but also, at the same time, this gradual escalation, I think, again, that the focus of this particular hearing is very useful. How do you break that cycle of provocations, given the trajectory that we see right now?

Rather than go down the rabbit's hole of trying to interpret North Koreans' intentions or explain why they do what they do, I think it's useful, in the short time I'm allotted today, to focus on what's different. What has changed in the region in particular vis-a-vis 2 or 3 years ago, that has either caused or perhaps enabled this recent escalation of North Korean provocations? I will make four short points in this regard.

First and foremost, I think the influence of, and the role of, the United States in this cycle of provocations is less than we may want to think. There is a very compelling narrative which holds each North Korean action is somehow "all about us," that they are reaching out to us, that they want talks for us. Unfortunately, if you look at the last 2 years, no matter what the action of North Korea, whether it is a charm offensive or an attack or a provocation of some other sort, they're always presumed to be influenced by the exact same motivating factor in North Korea, which is a desire to talk to the United States. I would think that domestic developments in North Korea, changes in inter-Korean relations, and changes in Chinese behavior have far greater explanatory power, in terms of understanding what is going on inside of North Korea right now.

The second major point I would make in this regard is precisely that the primary driver of North Korean actions, statements, and provocations is domestic, inside North Korea. I think Dr. Noland will address some of that quite well, following my remarks. While my assigned focus on the regional picture doesn't allow me to dwell on this in depth, I would point out that the more North Korean actions are linked to domestic developments in North Korea, and the more they're linked, in particular, to the question of succession, the less influence we have on those, as the United States.

As such, I think our time today is well served on focusing on those areas where we do have greater influence. And I will spend the bulk of my short time focusing on two developments in particular, those in South Korea and those in China.

In that regard, the third point upon which I would focus is that the biggest change in the region, over the last 3 years in particular, has been a change in inter-Korean relations, and in particular a change in South Korean policy toward North Korea. We had 10 years of progressive governments in South Korea; two successive administrations who pursued a policy of sunshine and active— proactive engagement with North Korea, where they became a major source of fertilizer, of food, of economic assistance, and of outright cash. That policy has changed dramatically. And so, in many respects, I think what you see right now is that, after 3 years of a remarkably principled and consistent application of the Lee Myung-bak administration's approach to North Korea, you've seen North Korea vacillating back and forth between inducements or a charm offensive on the one hand, and on the other hand threats and outright provocations, in their openly stated attempt to break the Lee Myung-bak policy.

The other factor that is related directly to South Korea has been a historic and commendable amount of close coordination and cooperation between the United States and South Korea, which also includes Japan as a United States ally. Secretary Campbell addressed this, but I think that that level of such coordination is historic. I think it has served us very well. Unfortunately, as we are consistent, that consistency itself has been a factor in the rising cycle of North Korean provocations, precisely because of that pendulum-swing. When one day inducements do not work, North Korea returns to provocations. I'm sorry to say that the failure of the North/South military-to-military talks, at the preliminary level a couple weeks ago now, do not bode well for where we are going. In fact, just in the last 2 days, we've seen a new round of North Korean vitriolic and threats coming out. That pendulum-swing, in some respects, is the very definition of the cycle. President Obama has repeatedly declared his intention to break that pattern of behavior. If we go back into negotiations in response to those threats, then obviously we're back in the cycle.

I would argue, in some respects, for the last 2 years, and from—in the North/South perspective, for the last 3 years—that we really have broken that cycle. That cycle, that Senator Kerry so eloquently described, of us going back into negotiations in response to this escalation, really hasn't taken place. But, in that refusal to go back to the cycle, there is the inherent risk of further escalations. And I think that is the situation we are facing right now.

The final point I'll deal with, really, is what I think is perhaps the most important factor here, and the factor which has seen the biggest change. That is a change in Chinese behavior. If you look over the last 8 years, United States-China cooperation on North Korea has been a major factor or a major selling point for the importance of the United States-China relationship. During the bulk of the Bush administration and the early months of the Obama administration, such United States-China cooperation on North Korea was, again, a highlight. We cooperated very well in response to the missile tests in early 2009, and in the United Nations, in response to the nuclear test in early 2009, as well, agreeing, together, on a historic U.N. Security Council Sanctions Resolution in June 15, 2009.

Somehow, in the summer of 2009 or the early fall of 2009, that changed, in terms of China's perspective. And would argue that China, as a nation, has always had three "no"s, in regarding North Korea: no collapse, no nukes, and no war. And they've always tried to balance those three priorities in regards to the Korean Peninsula. But, beginning, I presume, with the questions of Kim Jong-il's health, his stroke, succession, economic problems in North Korea, Chinese leadership, I believe, has prioritized the question of "no collapse." They are more concerned about collapse in North Korea than the other issues.

As such, beginning in August 2009, China stopped cooperating with us actively on implementing sanctions resolutions. And, if you look over the last year and a half, they've been very proactive, in public, in their support of the North Korean regime. One immediate impact of that has been to encourage North Korea toward, I believe, further negative behavior.

For example, even after the sinking of the *Cheonan,* the Chinese leadership decided to double down on their bet on North Korea. President Hu Jintao hosted Kim Jong-il, not just once, but twice, and Chinese officials very publicly argued that theirs was the appropriate approach. In late October, Chinese diplomats were almost smug in their discussions with me about the rectitude of their approach, saying that, because they had publicly backed Kim Jong-il during this time of instability with a risk of collapse, that there had been no more nuclear tests, there had been no missile tests, and there had been no disruption of the G20 meetings in Seoul, in November.

Unfortunately for that approach, November of last year was a very bad month. The North Korean revalation of a uranium enrichment program, their construction of a new light-water nuclear reactor, and the shelling of Yeonpyeong Island, I think, exposed to all the impotence of, and the counterproductive nature of, the Chinese approach.

In a nutshell, I think that's a fundamental factor. That's something that is very different than was the situation 2 years ago. And that has to be addressed, as we look at how to break out of the cycle.

Let me just wrap up very quickly by looking at some of the implications for policy. First and foremost, I would say that there's a need to stay the course. If we are out of the cycle, indeed, right now, then the continued emphasis on close coordination and cooperation with our primary allies in the region—in this case, South Korea and Japan—is the foundation upon which any other approach will go. Second, based on the strength of that approach, we have to continue to convince China that its actions have been counterproductive to the stability of the overall region; that by emphasizing overly on avoiding a collapse in North Korea, they have actually caused the risk of war in the region to go up, and actually let the North Korean nuclear program to develop to a degree that it should not have.

Essentially, what we're asking China to do is, not to abandon its North Korean ally, but to recalibrate its prioritization.

I must say that the events in the Middle East in the last several weeks probably have reinforced the negative behavior and negative perceptions in China. And so, I'm not overly optimistic that China will recalibrate its approach. I would say that if China does not do that, I think, just as the President has said and Secretary Campbell said today, it is incumbent upon the United States to make sure that we work closely with our ally to respond to the provocations as they come, again, as a way of breaking out of the cycle.

The final point I will make is that I do think there is a wonderful roadmap for going forward, if we focus on it. During the summit meeting, between President Obama and President Hu in January of this year, there was only one paragraph in their joint statement which was dedicated to North Korea. But, in that one statement, three times they referenced the September 19, 2005, Joint Statement of the Six-Party Talks. I think that's extremely helpful, because what it has done is define what "denuclearization" means, it has defined the parameters of the six-party talks, and it has defined precisely what you, Chairman Kerry, asked, in terms of: What are the basic requirements of what North Korea needs to do to come back to talks? I'm hopeful that such definition will lead us going forward.

And I'll end my remarks there.

Thank you.

[The prepared statement of Mr. Flake follows:]

PREPARED STATEMENT OF L. GORDON FLAKE

BEYOND THE BILATERAL: UNDERSTANDING THE CHALLENGE OF NORTH KOREA IN A REGIONAL CONTEXT

One of the particular challenges in dealing with an opaque regime like North Korea is the difficulty in assessing the intentions or motivations behind particular policies or positions taken by the North Korean Government. Absent reliable information on North Korea's internal decisionmaking process, a common conceit in the United States is to assume that North Korean actions and statements are somehow "all about us," motivated by and targeted to an audience in the United States. Given the asymmetry of U.S. power globally, such assumptions are not limited to U.S. dealings with North Korea. Yet in the absence of alternative explanations from Pyongyang, this narrative often holds sway as analysts, journalists, and government officials alike attempt to interpret the most recent North Korean provocation or charm offensive.

The problem with this approach is that the conclusion drawn inevitably seems to be the same no matter what the North Korea action, and again it is all about us. Thus, North Korea's long-range missile tests and nuclear tests are purported to be attempts to force the United States into direct bilateral talks. Pyongyang's August 2009 decision to divest itself of two imprisoned U.S. journalists for the price of having former President Clinton pick them up is likewise seen as a sign of outreach to the United States, as was the decision to turn over the unfortunate Ajalon Gomes to former President Carter in August 2010.

More recently, in early November 2010 when North Korea showed separate delegations from the United States evidence of construction of a new light-water nuclear reactor and a surprisingly sophisticated uranium enrichment facility, calls for the United States to resume negotiations with North Korea were both immediate and predictable. Even after North Korea shelled the South Korean coastal island of Yeonpyeong on November 23, 2010, in a drastic and highly provocative escalation of the longstanding inter-Korean tensions in the West Sea, some Americans persisted in interpreting this action in context of United States-North Korean relations. For example, former President Jimmy Carter authored a New York Times op-ed entitled "North Korea Wants to Make a Deal"[1] following his August visit to Pyongyang. He again urged the U.S. to listen to "North Korea's Consistent Message to the U.S."[2] in a Washington Post op-ed that described the North's unprecedented provocation as "designed to remind the world that they deserve respect in negotiations" and repeated North Korea's insistence on "direct talks with the United States."

Of course, there are alternate if equally improbable interpretations of North Korean intentions or the motivations behind North Korean actions and statements. Given the fact that North Korea has now repeatedly declared itself a nuclear power and declared its intent to develop nuclear deterrence as well as nuclear energy, its decision to test nuclear weapons and to construct both a light-water nuclear reactor facility and a uranium enrichment facility might more logically be understood in the context of North Korea's stated intentions and goals. The notion that "all politics is local" is not only applicable to democracies. The Democratic People's Republic of Korea (DPRK) has made ample use of its nuclear tests and status in its internal propaganda and there is increasing evidence to suggest that with the continued de-

---

[1] http://www.nytimes.com/2010/09/16/opinion/16carter.html.
[2] http://www.washingtonpost.com/wp-dyn/content/article/2010/11/23/AR2010112305808.html.

cline of its conventional military capacity, chronic food shortages, and a moribund economy, the legitimacy of the Kim regime is increasingly tied to its nuclear status. This should weigh heavily on the decades-old debate as to whether the North Korean nuclear program is primarily—or at this point even possibly—a bargaining chip.

In addition to such domestic factors, North Korean actions are also far better understood in the context of the DPRK's more immediate relationships with its primary patron China and its chief rival, the Republic of Korea (ROK). Given the priority that China has placed upon the moribund six-party talks, it would be foolish not to interpret North Korea's reluctant references to the possibility of returning to such talks squarely in the context of Chinese demands. Likewise, given the relatively dramatic shift in South Korea's policy toward its northern neighbor after a decade of "sunshine" (during which the Government in ROK was a major source of food, fertilizer, and capital for the DPRK), many of Pyongyang's actions and statements are better explained by such immediate concerns than by any aspirations it might have vis-a-vis the United States. Accordingly, this testimony focuses primarily upon the regional context of recent North Korean actions and upon the importance of a regional approach to responding to developments in North Korea, regardless of their nature or direction. While Japan and Russia have and continue to play important roles related to North Korea and the six-party talks, this testimony focuses primarily on changes in South Korea and in China that are most directly related to the current cycle of North Korean provocations.

PENINSULAR PRIMACY: THE INTER-KOREAN DYNAMIC

The country with the most interest—and the most to lose—in increased tensions with North Korea is undeniably its neighbor to the south, the Republic of Korea. Changing political dynamics in South Korea are also one of the most important factors in understanding the changed inter-Korean political relationship. After the better part of four decades of inter-Korean relations defined primarily by ongoing hostility and deterrence, South Korea's policy toward the North shifted dramatically after the costs of German unification became readily apparent. Beginning with the inauguration of the Kim Dae-Jung administration in 1998, South Korea began to pursue a policy of "peaceful coexistence" with North Korea. This was followed by a policy of proactive engagement which was primarily manifest by the rather one-sided provisions of South Korean investment, fertilizer, and humanitarian aid to North Korea. This approach was initially intended to affect change in North Korea in the manner of Aesop's famed fable of "The North Wind and the Sun." However, over the next decade the primary objective of ROK policy toward North Korea, particularly during the Roh Moo-hyun administration, apparently shifted to one of ensuring stability in North Korea—at least in the short run.

While the South Korean Presidential election of 2007 was primarily a mandate on the management style and failings of the Roh administration, it was also somewhat of a referendum on President Roh's policy toward North Korea. Still, President Lee Myung-bak entered office espousing a long-term vision for inter-Korean relations that included significant South Korean investment in North Korea and a stated goal of dramatically increasing North Korean per capita GNP. This approach, however, was premised on changes in North Korean behavior, particularly on progress toward denuclearizing North Korea, an issue that had gained renewed salience following North Korea's October 9, 2006, test of a nuclear device. In practice, President Lee's policy was a sharp departure from that of his predecessors. The President and his advisers more openly raised issues such as North Korean human rights, participated in international efforts to curb North Korea's illicit activities, and changed they manner in which they handled development and humanitarian aid—all changes that were very unwelcome in Pyongyang.

In another respect, President Lee's approach to North Korea was at least in part a reflection of changing South Korean attitudes toward Pyongyang. Not only was there a growing sense that South Korea's decade of largess was unappreciated and unreciprocated, but during the first years of the Lee administration, a series of North Korean actions further influenced underlying South Korean public opinion and as a result Seoul's policy toward the North. On July 11, 2008, North Korean soldiers shot a South Korean tourist in the back at the Diamond Mountain resort. North Korea's subsequent refusal to engage in a joint investigation of the incident led to a shuttering of the Hyundai-Asan operated tourist zone. The fact that this event took place in the context of a North Korean long-range missile test and nuclear test on April 5 and May 25, 2009, respectively, further hardened South Korean public opinion. Despite these and subsequent events, South Korea has yet to pull its support from the Kaesong Industrial Complex, however the detention of a South

Korean employee for 137 days during the summer of 2009 further colored South Korean views of that project and the prospects for engagement with North Korea. Tensions again rose in the West Sea with a naval altercation[3] South Korea calls the "Battle of Daecheong" on November 10, 2009. This resulted in severe damage of a North Korean patrol boat and North Korean threats of retaliation, which may have found their realization in the sinking of the South Korean corvette the *Cheonan* on March 26, 2010.

While the sinking of the *Cheonan* and the tragic loss of 46 South Korean sailors shocked the South Korean public, initial uncertainty about the cause of the tragedy, the lengthy investigation, the fact that the incident took place out of sight and at night, and the fact that the initial findings of the investigation were announced shortly before South Korean local elections all served to make this particular incident politically divisive within South Korea. That was not the case with the November 23, 2010, shelling of Yeonpyeong Island. The North Korean artillery barrage took place in broad daylight, and if a picture is worth a thousand words, live video must certainly be worth many times more. Real time images of columns of smoke streaming skyward from the island as panicked refugees fled the scene served to affect the most fundamental shift in South Korean public opinion toward North Korea in over a decade. Suddenly President Lee Myung-Bak who in some circles was still considered to be a hard-liner was accused of failing to protect the nation and threatened with impeachment by some members of his party. President Lee, whose apparent first instinct and first statements focused on avoiding an escalation of the crisis, was gradually pushed by public outrage to revise the rules of engagement and to state clearly that any future such incidents would be met with a considerable show of force.

In this political context tensions on the Korea Peninsula rose dramatically in December 2010 with South Korea's decision to proceed with further live-fire exercises in the area surrounding Yeonpyeong Island in the face of North Korean threats to retaliate. While these exercises as well as joint U.S. and South Korean naval exercises went forth without immediate North Korean retaliation, it is useful to remember that North Korea's retaliation does not always take place at a time and place of the allies' choosing and tensions on the peninsula remain high. If the sinking of the *Cheonan* was indeed the promised North Korean response to the Battle of Daecheong 5 months earlier, U.S. and South Korean defense planners would be wise to watch for a similarly out of the blue, seemingly unprovoked response to Seoul's decision to continue its live-fire exercises in the face of North Korean threats.

Perhaps encouraged by Chinese pressure in advance of President Hu Jintao's January visit to Washington, Pyongyang began this year with calls for "unconditional" talks with South Korea. On the surface, this would seem to be a welcome development, particularly following the tensions surrounding the shelling of Yeonpyeong Island last November. However, even if one is inclined to take such diplomatic overtures from North Korea at face value, this offer is anything but "unconditional." To begin with, an unspoken condition of such talks was that South Korea ignore what were by almost any measure two recent acts of war by North Korea. Absent any reference to its actions, the North Korean offer of talks seems less like a sincere offer for negotiations and more like an attempt to cause political divisions in South Korea by casting itself as the willing party and the Lee Myung-bak administration as the obstacle to diplomacy.

The content of the talks proposed by North Korea provides further indication of its intentions. In the initial North Korean offer, there was scant mention of security issues, military-to-military dialogue, or North Korea's nuclear program. Instead, Pyongyang proposed to talk about economic cooperation with a transparent objective of seeking to renew the flow of South Korea aid and the cash that accompanied past cooperation. What North Korea has to gain from such talks is obvious, the benefit for South Korea is less clear. Even during the decade of engagement and summitry under two successive progressive governments in South Korea, Pyongyang steadfastly resisted recognizing South Korea as a legitimate partner for a meaningful dialogue on security issues on the peninsula including the armistice, a potential peace agreement, or North Korea's nuclear program.

---

[3] After nearly 50 years of relative quiet on the West Sea, in mid-1999 North Korea began a concerted effort to challenge the Northern Limit Line (NLL), which it has never officially recognized, but which has served as a de facto maritime border since the signing of the armistice. Of the many subsequent naval clashes along the NLL, it is worth noting that both the first and second "Battle Yeonpyeong" (June 15, 1999, and June 29, 2002) occurred despite the ROK's then-engagement policy toward the North.

In this context, North Korea's mid-January 2011 proposal for high-level military-to-military talks with the South was certainly a positive development. Given the events of the preceding months, South Korea responded cautiously and proposed preparatory talks in early February that broke off amidst mutual recriminations. Of note, the question of North Korea's nuclear program was not on the agenda, and South Korea's attempts to ensure that the *Cheonan* and Yeonpyeong Island incidents were on the agenda for the senior-level meeting appears to have been the primary area of dispute and the cause for breakdown of the talks. Despite the apparent stalemate, South Korean officials have repeatedly stated that an apology for the incidents is not a precondition nor is it formally linked to the resumption of six-party talks. While President Lee himself has repeatedly and recently emphasized his desire for talks with the North and resumption of the six-party talks, in the short-term progress on that front appears unlikely.

South Korea's changing approach to North Korea has also had a direct impact on United States-South Korean relations and upon the United States ability to coordinate its own policies toward North Korea. For example, much of the political difficulties experienced between Washington and Seoul during the tenure of President Roh Moo-hyun can be attributed to what were then rapidly diverging threat perceptions regarding North Korea. Over the past 3 years, due in part to the laundry list of provocations noted above, there has been a dramatic reconvergence in U.S. and ROK perceptions of North Korea. This alone, however, cannot explain the dramatic improvement in United States-ROK relations. The improvement began with the election of President Lee during the last year of the Bush administration and accelerated dramatically given the high priority the incoming Obama administration placed upon prior consultation and coordination with its ally Seoul on all matters regarding North Korea. The June 19, 2009, Joint Vision Statement for the U.S.-ROK Alliance[4] is a historic document. This, along with the Korea U.S.-Free Trade Agreement, the ROK role in and hosting of the G20, and its role in and hosting of the next Nuclear Security summit, lends substance to the claim that United States-ROK relations are the best that they have ever been.

The result of this convergence has been a remarkably principled, consistent, and well-coordinated policy between Seoul, Washington, and Tokyo in regards to North Korea. Historically both the U.S. and ROK approaches toward North Korea have vacillated, while North Korea has remained relatively consistent in its demands and intransigence. The inevitable failure of one approach has led successive democratic governments in both Seoul and Washington to try different approaches at different times over the past two decades. One need only contrast the vastly different approaches to North Korea during the first and second term of the Bush administration for evidence of this tendency.

Ironically, one of the most immediate causes of the most recent cycle of North Korean provocations may be the consistent and coordinated approach with which the Obama and the Lee administrations have responded to North Korea. President Obama has repeatedly framed the joint United States-ROK approach in the context of the need to "break the pattern" of responding to North Korean provocations with concessions and talks that do not make progress on core issues at hand. In response, it is North Korea that has vacillated between threats, inducements, provocations, charm offensives, and outright attacks in their attempt to force or cajole the U.S. and South Korea to abandon their current approach. While this approach may portend further tensions in the months ahead, to abandon principles at this point would be to surrender to the cycle.

CHINA: PARTNER OR PATRON

While somewhat simplistic, one way to understand Chinese priorities in North Korea is to focus upon the more negative scenarios that China clearly hopes to avoid on the peninsula. There are the three "no's"—no nukes, no collapse, and no war. China has long sought to balance what have oftentimes been competing priorities in this regard. For the better part of the past 8 years cooperation on addressing the challenges posed by North Korea and in particular the North Korean missile and nuclear programs has been a highlight of United States-China cooperation. A perfunctory review of official U.S. statements regarding China during the bulk of the Bush administration and the early months of the Obama administration will turn up a veritable mantra highlighting the importance of the United States-China relationship in working together on North Korea. Indeed, in the early months of the Obama administration, United States-China cooperation on North Korea reached its

[4] http://www.whitehouse.gov/the_press office/Joint-vision-for-the-alliance-of-the-United-States-of-America-and-the-Republic-of-Korea/.

arguable peak as, despite their initial misgivings, China supported a strongly worded Presidential statement at the U.N. Security Council in response to North Korea's testing of a long-range missile. Shortly thereafter, on June 12, 2009, China signed on to the most meaningful sanctions resolutions on North Korea to date, UNSC 1874.

While the exact cause of the shift is as of yet unknown, after initially cooperating with the United States and the international community in implementing these sanctions, beginning sometime around the early fall 2009 there appears to have been a marked shift in Chinese priorities and views on how best to address the North Korean problem. Not only did they scale back their cooperation on implementing the U.N. Security Council sanctions, but they also began to be overtly and actively supportive of the Kim Jong-il regime. One possible explanation is that given the concern over North Korean leader Kim Jong-il's health, the uncertainties surrounding the succession process in North Korea, and evidence of ongoing economic turmoil in North Korea, the Chinese leadership felt it necessary to place a higher priority on its objective of avoiding collapse in North Korea. Stepped-up Chinese support for North Korea continued over the fall, and even when faced with the sinking of the *Cheonan* in March 2010, the Chinese leadership decided to double their bet on the Kim Jong-il regime rather than altering course. Chinese President Hu Juntao met with Kim Jong-il not just once but twice in the aftermath of the *Cheonan* sinking and China repeatedly refused to hear evidence on or except conclusion that North Korea was responsible for this tragic event. As recently as October 2000 Chinese officials were almost smug in their assessment of the rectitude of their approach, noting with some satisfaction that since China had begun to seek an easing of pressure on North Korea and had become more overt in their backing for the Kim Jong-il regime, North Korea had not tested another nuclear weapon, had not tested another long-range missile and had not disrupted the G20 meetings with President Hu in Seoul.

This defense of the Chinese approach unraveled dramatically in November 2010 when in quick succession North Korea announced that it had begun construction of light-water nuclear reactor and showed a visiting U.S. delegation what appeared to be a uranium enrichment facility replete with 2000 centrifuges in three different cascades and what appeared to be highly sophisticated modern control facilities. These were both developments that were clearly in violation not only of three different sets of standing U.N. Security Council sanctions resolutions, but more specifically in violation of the September 19, 2005, joint statement of the six-party talks. These disturbing revelations were then capped by the North Korean shelling of Yeongpyeong Island, an act that killed two South Korean marines and two South Korean civilians. While North Korea claimed that its artillery barrage was in response to a South Korean live-fire exercise in the area earlier that morning, the shelling of the South Korean island marks the first time since the end of hostilities in the Korean war that artillery shells were fired and landed upon South Korean. Despite the dramatic and shocking nature of these activities, China once again prevaricated and called for calm on all sides.

It is notable that over the period of shifting Chinese priorities in regards to North Korea there has also been a shift in U.S. views of China's role, beginning with disappointment over Chinese implementation of UNSC sanctions resolutions that China has voted for. By the summer of 2010 these concerns were expressed as criticisms of China's willful ignorance of North Korean behavior. U.S. views shifted further still following the most recent revelations regarding North Korea's nuclear program and its November artillery barrage. China was openly accused of "enabling" North Korean bad behavior—the implication being that China's decision to shield North Korea from the consequences of its actions was at least in part responsible for the continuation of such provocations. Secretary of State Clinton perhaps said it best when, immediately prior to the Obama-Hu summit, she openly questioned whether China's failure to respond to the sinking of the South Korean corvette was not in some way responsible for the North Korean willingness to go forward with its artillery barrage: "We fear and have discussed this in depth with our Chinese friends, that failure to respond clearly to the sinking of a South Korean military vessel might embolden North Korea to continue on a dangerous course. The attack on Yeonpyeong Island that took the lives of civilians soon followed." [5] In short, after the better part of a decade of being viewed as part of the solution to North Korea there is a growing concern that absent a readjustment of its priorities, China is increasingly part of the problem.

---

[6] http://www.theglobeandmail.com/news/world/americas/prepared-text-of-clintons-speech/article1870858/.

In this context, there was particular importance placed upon the January summit meeting between President Obama and Chinese President Hu Jintao. While there were obviously many issues to be addressed in the summit meeting given the risk of conflict on the Korean Peninsula and the proximity of recent attacks, it is safe to presume that North Korea was a high priority in discussions. While for his part President Hu could not muster a willingness to even mention North Korea by name—preferring instead to refer obliquely to the "Korean Peninsula issue" or the "Korean nuclear problem"—there was some evidence of progress, at least in examining how the issue was framed.

While it may seem arcane, there is some cause for optimism to be found in the single paragraph of the joint statement issued by President.

> The United States and China agreed on the critical importance of maintaining peace and stability on the Korean Peninsula as underscored by the joint statement of September 19, 2005, and relevant U.N. Security Council Resolutions. Both sides expressed concern over heightened tensions on the Peninsula triggered by recent developments. The two sides noted their continuing efforts to cooperate closely on matters concerning the Peninsula. The United States and China emphasized the importance of an improvement in North-South relations and agreed that sincere and constructive inter-Korean dialogue is an essential step. Agreeing on the crucial importance of denuclearization of the Peninsula in order to preserve peace and stability in Northeast Asia, the United States and China reiterated the need for concrete and effective steps to achieve the goal of denuclearization and for full implementation of the other commitments made in the September 19, 2005, joint statement of the six-party talks. In this context, the United States and China expressed concern regarding the DPRK's claimed uranium enrichment program. Both sides oppose all activities inconsistent with the 2005 joint statement and relevant international obligations and commitments. The two sides called for the necessary steps that would allow for early resumption of the Six-Party Talks process to address this and other relevant issues.[6]

In that short statement the September 19, 2005, joint statement of the six-party talks was mentioned three times. Such a reference to an obscure unimplemented agreement of talks that increasingly appeared defunct may seem a bit odd. However, one of the fundamental challenges of dealing with North Korea has been its frequent and continued assertion that it is a nuclear power and must be dealt with as such. When North Korea makes vague references to its support of denuclearization, its definition of denuclearization should be clarified and challenged. The apparent North Korean interpretation is that, as a nuclear power and an equal with the United States and the other nuclear powers in the world, it is willing to discuss the denuclearization of the Korean Peninsula, including the removal of the U.S. nuclear umbrella, the end of the United States-ROK alliance, and overall global disarmament of other nuclear powers' positions. This interpretation understandably is not acceptable to the United States, China, any other member of the six-party talks, or ostensibly any other signatory of the Nuclear Nonproliferation Treaty (NPT) (from which North Korea is the only country in history to withdraw). As such, a clear reference to the September 19, 2005, joint statement in which North Korea committed to "abandoning all nuclear weapons and existing nuclear programs and returning, at an early date, to the Treaty on the Non-Proliferation of Nuclear Weapons and to IAEA safeguards"[7] helps set a clear definition of what the U.S. and China now jointly mean when we refer to "denuclearization" including the denuclearization of the Korean Peninsula. Related to this is the question of the parameter of the six-party talks. With the September 19 joint statement the six-party talks are now more than format, but also have function and content. Given that in the joint statement "the six parties unanimously reaffirmed that the goal of the six-party talks is the verifiable denuclearization of the Korean Peninsula in a peaceful manner," by focusing upon this joint statement the U.S. and China once again jointly defined the parameters of—and indirectly a core requirement for—the resumption of the six-party talks. Also of note, the January 19, 2011, Obama-Hu joint statement also placed U.S. and Chinese "concern regarding the DPRK's claimed uranium enrichment program" clearly in the context of the September 19, 2005, joint statement.

Despite what appears to have been some progress during the January summit, there is at present some frustration at China's apparent refusal to allow the U.N. Security Council to take up the question of the North Korea uranium enrichment

---

[6] http://www.whitehouse.gov/the-press-office/2011/01/19/us-china-joint-statement.
[7] http://www.state.gov/p/eap/regional/c15455.htm.

program. Given the clarity of this issue and its importance to the broader objective on denuclearization, China's current position is if anything difficult to understand and will be a key indicator of China's role going forward.

Few analysts realistically expect China to abandon its erstwhile North Korean ally or to be proactive in putting major pressure on Pyongyang. However, at a minimum it is reasonable to expect China to recalibrate its position to make sure that it recognizes that in the process of trying to avoid collapse in North Korea, its approach to North Korea is actually increasing the risk of conflict and the likelihood of the further advancement of North Korea's nuclear program. At this point the key contribution China could make toward helping break the cycle of North Korean provocations would be to simply stop shielding North Korea from the consequences of its actions. In no small part, the current cycle of North Korean provocations has been abetted by, if not encouraged by, apparently unconditional support from China.

CONCLUSION

The particular focus of this hearing is helpful in that it distinguishes between the much longer term task of solving the myriad issues related to North Korea and its inherent insecurity and the more immediate task of breaking free of the current cycle of North Korean provocations. Any effort to seriously address the recent cycle of North Korean provocations must begin with an attempt to understand the root causes of North Korean actions.

Although these causes cannot be fully addressed in this testimony, there is disturbing evidence that suggests that much of the current crisis in North Korea is related to internal developments inside North Korea. Following Kim Jong-il's apparent stroke in 2008, the process of succession planning in North Korea appears to have been rushed. Given the multitude of economic, societal, and security challenges faced by the current regime in North Korea, the prospects for a smooth transition to a third generation of Kims appears daunting. As much as recent North Korean provocations are directly related to the succession and the internal situation within North Korea, they may simply be beyond our control. Just as recent events in the Middle East have demonstrated the limits of American influence, even in countries where we have overriding national security interests, so too are there very real limitations on our ability to directly influence ongoing dynamics within Pyongyang.

However, given that the primary context—and in some cases facilitation—of many recent North Korean actions lies firmly in the countries bordering North Korea, understanding this dynamic and working together with American allies and other partners in the region offers the best hope of breaking the cycle of North Korean provocations.

On a regional level, there are two factors most directly related to North Korea's most recent cycle of provocation. First and foremost is the change in South Korean policy toward the North, which now deprives the North of key inputs to its economy and government upon which the DPRK had come to rely. Related to this factor is, of course, the remarkably well-coordinated approach between the United States, South Korea and Japan and the consistency with which this approach has been applied in response to North Korean actions. In some respects, the pendulum swing of North Korean provocations and diplomatic initiatives is an indication of the success of this approach. Perversely, however, if the United States and its allies are serious about "breaking the pattern" of North Korean negotiating behavior, there are inherent risks of escalation and miscalculation related to that approach.

The best way to mitigate such risks is to ensure as close as possible coordination with all other partners in the region. Here lies the second factor related to the current escalatory cycle—China's increased support for Pyongyang despite North Korean actions. This is not to shift full responsibility to China or to imply that China has either the will or the capacity to somehow "solve" the North Korean problem. But in the current context there is ample evidence to suggest that China's efforts to avoid the downside risk of instability in North Korea are at least in part responsible for enabling recent North Korean provocations, thereby increasing the risk of conflict. China's disproportionate focus on internal stability in North Korea has made a challenge related to North Korea's nuclear program infinitely more complex.

China has already clearly demonstrated that, left to its own devices, it is prepared to tolerate, if not actively support, the North Korean regime despite the downside risks as long as it can avoid instability. This is a tendency within China that is likely stronger today after the dramatic events of the past month in the Middle East.

The question is thus how best might the United States and its allies influence Chinese decisionmaking. While there is no easy answer, the importance of a unified approach cannot be overstated. The U.S. and its allies must continue to as clearly as possible make the case to China that North Korea's actions are detrimental to the stability of the region and to China's own strategic national interests. As long as China is not willing to cooperate and continues to shield North Korea from the consequences of its actions, the U.S. and its allies should make clear that they must prepare to respond to likely future North Korean provocations outside of the context of coordination with China, a scenario which is in no one's interest.

While this conclusion may appear stark, it is also firmly grounded in the political realities of a crisis with North Korea that appears to offer fewer options with each passing day. For example, a fundamental precondition for resumption of the six-party talks is a willingness on North Korea's part to abandon its assertion that it is a nuclear power. In their January 19 joint summit statement, President Obama and President Hu rightly defined that precondition as adherence to the September 19, 2005, joint statement of the six-party talks. Put simply, if China continues to bolster the North Korean regime, there is little hope that North Korea will make the minimum necessary compromises for resumption of meaningful dialogue. At the same time, given the severity of the acts perpetrated against South Korea, the United States cannot help but be supportive of its allies, and the underlying fact remains that it is impossible to conceive of progress in the six-party talks framework or even in a bilateral United States-North Korea talks absent meaningful progress in North-South relations.

In this process it is always useful to step back and remember that the United States fundamental strategic interests in Northeast Asia are the peace, prosperity, and economic progress of the region as a whole. In some respects, North Korea is best understood as the hole in the Northeast Asian donut. Our first priority is rightly placed on strengthening our alliance relationships in the region. Based upon a foundation of strong relations with Japan and Korea, the United States has considerably more influence with China and Russia than it would have otherwise. Likewise, the United States and its allies have a shared interest in ensuring that no matter what happens in North Korea—whether it collapses, instigates further conflict or, more hopefully, chooses a different path—that North Korea does not become an issue of contestation or conflict in the region more broadly.

The CHAIRMAN [presiding]. Thank you very much.

Dr. Noland.

## STATEMENT OF DR. MARCUS NOLAND, DEPUTY DIRECTOR, PETERSON INSTITUTE FOR INTERNATIONAL ECONOMICS, WASHINGTON, DC

Dr. NOLAND. Thank you. It's an honor to appear before this committee this morning.

I have provided a written statement to be entered into the formal hearing record.

I would like to make four basic points.

The growing centrality of markets in the North Korean economy over the past two decades is primarily due to state failure, not proactive reform.

The market is emerging as a semiautonomous zone of social communication and potentially political organizing. And, on its own terms, the state is right to fear the market. It's this fear of the market that prevents the North Korean authorities from embracing the sorts of economic reforms that would allow them to address their chronic food problems, which appear to be worsening.

One aspect of the economy's unplanned marketization has been the substantial growth in cross-border exchange, particularly with China, which now accounts for a rising share of North Korean trade. China, however, appears utterly uninterested in implementing sanctions in response to North Korean provocations.

The tragedy of North Korea is, the government is almost wholly unaccountable for its manifest failures, and has an almost unlimited capacity for inflicting misery on its people. Under such circumstances, conditional on agreement on procedural protocols, resumption in humanitarian aid is warranted. It is reasonable, however, to require greater policy conditionality on broader forms of engagement.

While attention is understandably focused on the high diplomacy of the nuclear issue, it's worthwhile to examine what is going on beneath the surface, as well. Research derived from large-scale surveys of refugees, as well as surveys of Chinese businesses doing business in North Korea, document a society characterized by growing inequality, criminality, and corruption. A significant share of the North Korean population has effectively delinked from the state and now exists in a kind of Hobbesian market economy.

And, paradoxically, while the state provides increasingly meager benefits to its population, contact with the state apparatus has grown ever more intimate. The government has undertaken legal code changes, which have effectively criminalized much of daily economic life, and facilitated the use of the penal system for extortion. In addition to its traditional role as an instrument of political repression, the penal system now serves as a mechanism for economic predation on the population, as well.

North Koreans have increasing access to foreign media sources. And, importantly, inhibitions against consuming foreign media have disappeared. As a consequence of obviously self-inflicted catastrophe, such as the failed currency reform, as well as increasing exposure to foreign media, the regime's meta-narrative, which ascribes all the country's problems to hostile foreign forces, is increasingly disbelieved. But, the society remains atomized and characterized by low levels of trust. While discontent is almost surely widespread, there appears to be an almost complete absence of civil society institutions capable of channeling that dissent into effective political action. And while overt demands for political change go unarticulated, the state retains a massive apparatus to compel compliance.

North Korea experienced a famine in the 1990s that killed perhaps 3 to 5 percent of the population, and has experienced chronic food shortages since. At present the food situation appears to be deteriorating as a result of an expected decline in domestic harvests, together with North Korean provocations and rising world food prices, which have contributed to a reduction in both aid and commercial imports. Prices are rising rapidly, internally, and a consortium of U.S. NGOs has now produced a firsthand assessment, which documents acute malnutrition among children and low-birth-weight newborns.

The North Korean Government has never exhibited any real buy-in to the norms of humanitarian assistance, as practiced elsewhere around the world, and establishing acceptable terms for a humanitarian aid program remains an ongoing challenge.

Historically, North Korea's international trade was small and politically determined. But, a byproduct of the famine and the unplanned marketization of the economy has been an expansion of decentralized trade, particularly with China, which in 2009 accounted for approximately 35 percent of North Korean trade, a figure that is likely to rise in 2010, once the data are available.

As in the case of the domestic market economy, the North Korean regime does not appear entirely comfortable with this phenomenon of decentralized border exchange. And the government appears to be attempting to execute a highly controlled opening, in which North Korean state organs would engage in cross-border commerce with China, but activities not controlled by the state would be quashed. And, as I indicated earlier, the Chinese have shown no interest in enforcing U.N. sanctions on North Korea.

North Korea's chronic food insecurity once again appears to be worsening. Externally, the country is increasingly relying on China, which is reluctant to sanction North Korea in response to its provocations. The regime faces a looming succession, driven by Kim Jong-il's age and health. Surveys document widespread discontent among the North Korean people, but also a dearth of civil-society institutions capable of channeling that mass discontent into constructive political action.

Access to information plays an essential political role. Connecting individuals to the outside world serves a crucial function of undermining state propaganda, thereby encouraging the government to respond to a more informed public. In this context, the market represents a zone of personal autonomy and freedom. We should be promoting its expansion through a process of engagement, but engagement with our eyes open. The goal would be not only to address North Korea's chronic material needs, but to also encourage economic and political evolution in constructive directions.

Information and markets alone will not immediately transform the North Korean regime. But, they are a start. The expansion of the market internally, exposure of more North Koreans to new sources of information, new ways of doing business and organizing their lives, even exposure to foreign countries, will foster conditions amenable to the North Korean people exerting greater constraints on the behavior of what is now an effectively unaccountable regime.

Thank you.

[The prepared statement of Dr. Noland follows:]

### PREPARED STATEMENT OF DR. MARCUS NOLAND

The North Korean regime resembles a surfer attempting to maintain his balance on top of a changing, unstable foundation. While attention has understandably focused on the nuclear issue, it is worthwhile to examine the wave as well as the surfer to understand how the ride may end.

I would like to make three basic points:

- The growing centrality of markets in the North Korean economy over the past two decades is primarily due to state failure, not proactive reform. The market is emerging as a semiautonomous zone of social communication and, potentially, political organizing. On its own terms, the state is right to fear the market.
- This fear of the market prevents the North Korean authorities from embracing economic reforms that would allow them to address their chronic food problems, which appear to be worsening.
- One aspect of the economy's unplanned marketization has been a substantial growth in cross-border exchange, particularly with China, which accounts for a rising share of North Korean trade. China appears utterly uninterested in implementing sanctions in response to North Korean provocations. In turn, North Korean authorities are attempting to recentralize trade, eliminating the decentralized market-oriented participants, and replacing them with intermediaries subject to greater direct political control.

The tragedy of North Korea is that while the circumstances of many are abysmal the government is almost wholly unaccountable for its manifest failures.

CHANGING ECONOMIC PRACTICES AND MORES

North Korea historically has been a planned economy. The growing centrality of markets over the last two decades is best interpreted as a product of state failure, most conspicuously with respect to the famine in the 1990s that killed perhaps 3–5 percent of the population.[1] Since then policy has been ambivalent, sometimes acquiescing to facts on the ground, at other times attempting to roll back these developments. Since roughly 2004–05, the policy trend has been negative or illiberal, prioritizing control over deepening or extending reform. A failed November 2009 currency reform and the government's subsequent backtracking destroyed an unknown share of household savings and accelerated inflation.[2] Against the backdrop of a failed agricultural policy and chronic food shortages, grain prices are again rising rapidly in part due to renewed military procurements and global market conditions.[3] Official state media has already begun to blame the rising prices on world markets.[4]

Research derived from two large-scale refugee surveys, involving more than 1,600 respondents, one conducted in China and the other in South Korea, suggest that in some sense a significant share of the population has effectively delinked from the state.[5] Many people derive most if not all of their income from market activities rather than employment in the state sector, and when we asked the refugees what was the best way to make money in North Korea, the majority responded "engage in market activities" but a growing number said "corrupt or criminal activities."

When asked about the best way to get ahead, the dominant response was state and party. But it appears that state positions are increasingly desired not out of patriotism but rather as a platform for corruption. Refugees who had formerly been employed in government or party offices reported increased corruption among their former colleagues. Similar accounts of corruption among state officials were reported by more than 300 Chinese businesses interviewed about their activities in North Korea.[6] The central authorities have responded by requiring party and government offices to devote more time to ideological indoctrination.

Paradoxically, while the state provides increasingly meager benefits to the population, contact with the state apparatus has grown ever more intimate. The government has undertaken legal code changes that have in effect criminalized much of daily economic life and facilitated the use of the penal system for economic predation. The police are given extraordinary discretion with respect to whom to arrest and detain, and conditions in detention facilities where many of these "economic criminals" are confined are horrific, rivaling those in felony prisons and the political gulag.

This system is a perfect instrument for extortion. The police can arbitrarily place individuals and their families in institutions where beatings, torture, and death in custody occur regularly. Unsurprisingly, people will pay bribes to avoid getting entangled in this system. In short, in addition to its traditional role as an instrument of political repression, the penal system now serves as a mechanism for economic predation as well.

POTENTIAL POLITICAL IMPLICATIONS

North Koreans have increasing access to foreign media sources, and importantly, inhibitions against consuming foreign media have disappeared. As a consequence of obviously self-inflicted catastrophes such as the failed currency reform, as well as increasing exposure to foreign media, the regime's meta-narrative, which ascribes all the country's problems to hostile foreign forces, is increasingly disbelieved.

But the society remains atomized, characterized by low levels of trust. Even among the refugees, a self-selected group expected to have both more negative views of the regime and a lower aversion to risk than the remaining resident population,

---

[1] Stephan Haggard and Marcus Noland, "Famine in North Korea: Markets, Aid, and Reform" (Columbia University Press, 2007).

[2] Stephan Haggard and Marcus Noland, "The Winter of Our Discontent: Pyongyang Attacks the Market," Policy Briefs in International Economics 10–1 (Washington: Peterson Institute for International Economics, 2010).

[3] Stephan Haggard and Marcus Noland, "Food Prices. Monetary Policy, and Currency Reform (It's More Interesting Than It Sounds)," January 28, 2011, http://www.piie.com/blogs/nk/?p=89.

[4] Stephan Haggard and Marcus Noland, "A Hostile Environment? The Case of Food," February 17, 2011, http/www.piie.com/blogs/nk/?p=338.

[5] Stephan Haggard and Marcus Noland, "Witness to Transformation: Refugee Insights into North Korea" (Washington: Peterson Institute for International Economics, 2011).

[6] Stephan Haggard, Jennifer Lee, and Marcus Noland, "How China-North Korea Trade Works," February 19, 2011, http://www.piie.com/blogs/nk/?p=351.

only a minority reported having discussed or joked with their peers about their circumstances while in North Korea. But this may be changing.

Participation in market activities is associated with a cluster of characteristics:

- A greater likelihood to cite "political" motives for emigration;
- A 50-percent higher likelihood of being arrested;
- Distinctly negative views of the regime and crucially;
- A greater propensity to communicate those views to peers.

In short, the market is emerging as a semiautonomous zone of social communication and, potentially, political organizing. When asked at a recent event what North Koreans are talking about in the market, former U.K. Ambassador to North Korea, John Everhard, responded, "Egypt." [7]

The question naturally arises as to how representative the refugees are of the remaining resident population. At some level this is unanswerable—there are no public opinion surveys in North Korea. But extensive multivariate statistical testing of the results suggest that while the raw pool of respondents may oversample individuals with demographic characteristics or life experiences predisposing them to hold negative views, the hypothesis that the results obtained adequately represent the remaining resident population cannot be rejected statistically. And the results line up with those reported from other sources such as the survey of Chinese businesses, which are not subject to the same concerns regarding bias. In short, the survey results should be taken seriously.

While discontent is almost surely widespread, there appears to be an almost complete absence of civil society institutions capable to channeling dissent into effective political action. And while overt demands for political change go unarticulated, the state retains a massive apparatus to compel compliance.

THE FOOD SITUATION

North Korea suffers from chronic food shortages born of the state's pursuit of the understandable goal of food security through an inappropriate strategy of self-sufficiency. At present, driven by a variety of factors, the situation appears to be deteriorating.

Roughly two-thirds of the grain consumed in North Korea is produced locally, so the size of the domestic harvest matters for food security. The harvest, in turn, depends on both the weather and the availability of inputs such as fertilizer. During the last harvest cycle the weather was suboptimal, and North Korea's poor diplomatic relations with South Korea have resulted in a reduction in South Korean aid, in terms of both food and agricultural inputs. Although the United Nations' Food and Agriculture Organization (FAO) estimated that the 2010 fall harvest was slightly above the previous year's, the 2011 spring harvest is now expected to be significantly lower than initially projected, so that heading into the "lean months" of mid-2011, domestically produced supply will be down relative to the previous year.

North Korea receives food aid bilaterally from China and South Korea and multilaterally through the World Food Programme (WFP), to which the United States is the largest donor. Imports on commercial terms are limited. However, both commercial imports and aid are affected by global prices, which are now rising. Higher world prices are likely to contribute to a reduction of commercial imports.

Aid could be affected as well. There is an understandable tendency to interpret aid policy as a function of diplomatic maneuvering and as a consequence ignore the role of domestic political considerations in determining outcomes. A Chinese reduction in aid in 1993, undertaken in response to rising grain prices at home, was the proverbial straw that broke the camel's back and sent North Korea into famine. A similar episode played out in December 2007, when in response to rapidly rising grain prices, China embargoed exports, including those to North Korea, contributing to the biggest intensification of hunger since the end of the famine period.[8] The current backdrop of rising world grain prices does not augur well for the availability of external supply via any channel.

Local prices appear to be rising much more rapidly than world prices, however, possibly due to high levels of inflation in the wake of the failed currency reform, as well as removal of supply from the market to restock inventories maintained by the North Korean military and possibly to build up inventories for political celebrations.

[7] Ambassador John Everhard, "The Markets of Pyongyang," Korea Economic Institute of America, Washington, February, 2, 2011.

[8] Stephan Haggard and Marcus Noland, "Famine in North Korea Redux?" Journal of Asian Economics (September 2009): 384–95.

It is impossible to know with any precision what this means for food security. The FAO/WFP balance sheet exercises are flawed and at the aggregate level overstate the actual level of distress. Additionally, these balance sheet exercises ignore inventory destocking or accumulation, which can have large immediate effects on supplies actually available on the market, in either direction. If recent reports are to be believed, the impact of such activities are likely to be in the direction of reducing effective supply.

Moreover, the distribution of food insecurity is highly uneven in North Korea, both geographically and socioeconomically, and even apparently adequate supply at the macro level may disguise what could be severe distress in specific locales or among particular population groups. A recent assessment by a consortium of American nongovernmental organizations (NGOs) reports intensifying distress in three provinces which were visited.[9] Among other things, the report documents cuts in rations delivered by the government run rationing system; extraordinary shares of household income devoted to the purchase of food; and eyewitness accounts of acute malnutrition among children and a prevalence of low birth-weight newborns.

Unfortunately, the North Korean Government has never exhibited any real "buy-in" to the norms of humanitarian assistance as practiced elsewhere around the world. As a consequence of this fundamental lack of cooperation by the recipient government, the quality of the official multilateral aid program in North Korea has never met international standards. Anecdotal accounts suggest that relative to the WFP, the American NGOs were able to achieve a higher level of effectiveness during their involvement in 2008. Recent North Korean provocations have further undercut political support among major donors, with the possible exception of China. In short, the food situation in North Korea appears to be deteriorating once again, though our understanding remains limited and as does our confidence in the quality of the aid program.

The ultimate solution to North Korea's chronic food insecurity is a revitalization of the North Korean economy, which would allow the country to earn foreign exchange and purchase bulk grains from more efficient producers worldwide. The regime is reluctant to embrace the reforms necessary to achieve this outcome, however, and if anything, economic policy is heading in a negative direction.

## EXTERNAL ECONOMIC RELATIONS

Historically, North Korea's international trade has been small and politically determined. A byproduct of the famine was the development of decentralized trade, mostly with China, which arose as a wide variety of organizations including work units, local government and party offices, and even military units initially engaged in barter transactions to secure grain, a process that eventually broadened to include monetized transactions over a wide range of products. In 2009 China accounted for approximately 35 percent of North Korean trade, a figure that will likely rise when data are available, insofar as bilateral trade expanded in 2010, while North Korea's trade with other partners appears to have stagnated. (One sometimes reads accounts that attribute to China 70 or 80 percent of North Korea's trade; these statements involve a fundamental misunderstanding of the data.)[10]

As in the case of the domestic market economy, the North Korean regime does not appear to be entirely comfortable with this phenomenon of decentralized cross-border exchange, which potentially poses profound challenges to the North Korean leadership. When economic circumstances deteriorate, the incentives rise to move into China either permanently or in search of business opportunities and food. Informal trade channels became important means of earning foreign exchange and financing much-needed imports. This movement and trade eroded the government's monopoly on information about the outside world. Cross-border trade has also come to include an array of communications and cultural products, which directly undermine the government's monopoly on information: from small televisions capable of receiving Chinese broadcasts in border areas to South Korean videos and DVDs and even mobile phones. In response to these developments, in recent months the government appears to be attempting to execute a highly controlled opening in which North Korean state organs would engage in cross-border commerce with China, but activities not controlled by the state would be quashed.

In parallel, the government has established a supra-cabinet body called the Joint Venture Investment Committee to act as a central approvals agency for all incoming

---

[9] Penelope Anderson and David Austin, "Rapid Food Security Assessment Democratic People's Republic of Korea," February 22, 2011.

[10] Marcus Noland, "Just How Big are Those Lips and Teeth?" February 10, 2011, http://www.piie.com/blogs/nk/?p=281.

investment. It is possible that this "one-stop shop" could serve as a mechanism for disciplining the cascading corruption at all levels that has deviled foreign investors. However, the centralization of control may also simply serve to channel bribery in politically approved directions, and as such, the composition of the group could be read as a map of power relationships within the regime. The committee is reportedly chaired by Ri Chol, a former North Korean Ambassador to Switzerland, who in his 30 years there was reputed to have been involved in the deposit in Swiss institutions of Kim family wealth, as well as the Swiss schooling of two of Kim Jong-il's sons.[11] Similarly, the Korea Taepung International Investment Group, whose board is chaired by a Korean-Chinese with commercial ties to the North Korean military but otherwise consists of regime heavyweights, was awarded a central place in the recently announced 10-year development plan, which notionally includes large Chinese investments in the Rason area in extreme northeastern North Korea. The government has also established a State Development Bank, reputedly at Chinese urging. These moves could be interpreted as indicating a renewed commitment to economic development and/or as a means of disciplining corrupt practices that have deterred investment. But there are also examples from other post-communist economies where such centralization has been accompanied by an increase in corruption, typically to the benefit of the leader, his family, and close associates.

## CONCLUSIONS

North Korea's chronic food insecurity once again appears to be worsening. Externally, the country is increasingly reliant on China, which is reluctant to sanction North Korea in response to its provocations. The regime faces a looming succession driven by Kim Jong-il's age and health. Our surveys document widespread discontent among the North Korean people but also a dearth of civil society institutions capable of channeling that mass discontent into constructive political action.

Access to information plays an essential political role. All societies, even democracies, are vulnerable to government propaganda and misinformation. But in closed societies, authoritarian governments have particular leeway to develop elaborate propaganda machines that fundamentally distort information about the outside world. Connecting individuals to the outside world serves the crucial function of undermining these distortions by providing information, encouraging the government to respond to a more informed public. Our surveys suggest that the North Korean public is receptive to alternative, non-state-controlled sources of information that not only expand freedom of thought but potentially increase capabilities as well.

In this context, the market represents a zone of personal autonomy and freedom. We should be promoting its expansion through a process of engagement—but engagement with our eyes open. The goal would be not only to address North Korea's chronic material needs but also to encourage economic and political evolution in constructive directions.

Humanitarian aid should be divorced from politics. We should not punish poor families in Chongjin or school children in Wonsan for the behavior of a government over which they have no influence. In practical terms this puts us back in the slog of trying to achieve the best outcomes possible given the fundamentally uncooperative stance of the North Korean Government. We appear to care more about vulnerable North Koreans than their own government does.

Development assistance is a different matter, however, and policy conditionality is justified. And while development assistance will be a component of an eventual reconstruction of the North Korean economy under whatever political circumstances prevail, official aid alone will be not be sufficient. Bringing prosperity to North Korea will require the establishment of a principled and sustainable basis for commercial engagement. This outcome, in turn, depends first and foremost on the stance of the North Korean Government, and recent developments in this regard have not been auspicious.

Information and markets alone will not immediately transform the North Korean regime. But they are a start. The expansion of the market internally, exposure of more North Koreans to new sources of information, new ways of doing business and organizing their lives, even exposure to foreign countries, will foster conditions amenable to the North Korean people exerting greater constraints on the behavior of what is now an effectively unaccountable regime.

---

[11] Yonhap, North Korea Newsletter no. 142, January 27, 2011, http://english.yonhapnews.co.kr/northkorea/2011/01/26/52/0401000000AEN20110126010400325F.HTML.

The CHAIRMAN. How do you get that exposure?

Dr. NOLAND. How do I get the——

The CHAIRMAN. Yes. I mean, it sounds good, but how do you—how are you going to do that—create the exposure of the North Korean people to these other things?

Dr. NOLAND. What we should be doing is encouraging North Korean Government to get involved in institutions, such as the World Bank. When those institutions are formulating their economic policies, there should be an attempt to put an emphasis on engagement with these sort of—I don't want to call them "nonstate institutions," because that would be an exaggeration, but these economic actors that are effectively operating outside central government control.

The CHAIRMAN. Why would they do that?

Dr. NOLAND. They don't want to do that, that's for sure. And the question is——

The CHAIRMAN. Well, what leverage do we have to get them to do that? I mean, I'm not sure where that beginning begins.

Dr. NOLAND. It begins in their current deteriorating conditions. They are faced with a situation——

The CHAIRMAN. It seems to me—I mean, listening to both Mr. Carlin and Mr. Flake, I get a sense that we're really misinterpreting what our interests are, vis-a-vis them and how they view us. And, if we are—if indeed everything they're doing is regime-survival-based and stability-based—and it seems, listening to Mr. Carlin, that they're not particularly concerned about talking to us or being engaged with us; they're kind of happy moving along and doing what they're doing—where does our leverage come from?

Dr. NOLAND. I think——

The CHAIRMAN. Am I——

Dr. NOLAND [continuing]. The way——

The CHAIRMAN [continuing]. Misinterpreting what you said, incidentally?

Mr. CARLIN. A little bit.

The CHAIRMAN. A little bit. OK. Well, correct me. I mean, I got a sense that you were saying that we're sort of presuming they want to talk to us, and that we're kind of going along this track of assumptions we're making that are incorrect.

Mr. CARLIN. Then I apologize if I was unclear. I think they are interested in talking to us, maybe less so than they were several years ago, but that, as you have suggested, until we sit down and explore what's possible, we can't know. We can't make assumptions, because, in fact, there is a track record. There is a history of a period when they were deeply engaged with us. And there's always a possibility we could get back to something like that again.

The CHAIRMAN. Yes, Mr. Flake.

Mr. FLAKE. The broader question of getting information into North Korea is a very important one. While I would agree with Dr. Noland about the utility of trying to do that on a government level, the truth is, the real game is inter-Korean, at this point. In fact, if you saw the media yesterday and this morning, there is considerable North Korean angst about South Koreans sending weather balloons over to North Korea with propaganda leaflets, which is kind of a small scale way to do it. But, the greater factor is that there are now 20,000 North Korean defectors living in South Korea who are pumping back money and information to their relatives all throughout North Korea; and probably double/triple that number in China, doing something very similar. You now have information flows in North Korea that you've never had before. And that's a fundamentally different dynamic than we were facing 20 years ago. And it's a destabilizing dynamic for the regime, which is, I think, again, part and parcel, wrapped up with the succession and other instability issues, an explanatory factor in looking at their recent provocations.

The CHAIRMAN. So, you were going to say—yes, Dr. Noland.

Dr. NOLAND. What I was going to say is, if they had the capacity, if they had the resources, yes, they would shut everything down. Everything would be centrally controlled. And they would be back in the world of the 1970s. That's what they would like to do. They don't have that capacity.

When the economy begins to deteriorate, they are forced, out of necessity, to allow a certain loosening up of the system. That's one dynamic. The other is, they're growing increasingly reliant on China, which can't make them comfortable.

So, while their preference clearly would be to exist in a world in which they could exert unlimited control both internally and in the organization of their external relations, there are internal pressures for them to have a certain degree of flexibility in how they organize both their internal economy as well as their external relations.

The CHAIRMAN. So, would you all be in agreement that it's important to get to this initial discussion, at least on a bilateral basis, to explore what's possible in six-party talks? Or are the six-party talks more of a tool and less critical to determining where to go?

Mr. CARLIN. I'll say something that a lot of people may not agree with. But, I think the six-party talks are a dead-end. And I don't think we should focus a lot of our attention and emotional commitment to them. If they serve their purpose, well and good, but we need something else, and getting to bilateral faster is more important.

The CHAIRMAN. Well, actually, Mr. Carlin, I happen to agree with you. I think if they happen to work and there's something that—functions effectively, terrific. But, I think they've tied our hands, to some degree. And I think they've become sort of an outlier argument for not necessarily doing what we ought to be doing that's in our interest.

Mr. FLAKE. I think, to be very frank, the six-party talks are really not about the talks themselves. They are about whether or not we accept North Korea as a nuclear power. There is nothing magic about a big, round table with 30 people convened around it. The plenary of the six-party talks, itself, is a very inefficient format for negotiating. But, the problem is that the only forum in which we have a standing commitment, on North Korea's part, to denuclearize, unilaterally, is that September 19, 2005, Joint Statement of the Six-Party Talks.

As I mentioned, in my remarks—it might seem strange that both President Obama and President Hu spent so much time focusing on an arcane, unimplemented statement from talks which are moribund. And the reason is, in that statement, North Korea committed to its companions in the six-party talks, the other countries in the region, that they would abandon all nuclear weapons and all existing nuclear programs, and return, at an early date, to the IAEA and NPT. And the moment we say, "six-party talks are dead. We're giving up on them." We have de facto recognized their assertion that they are a nuclear power. We have granted them that status.

The fundamental challenge of negotiating with North Korea, no matter what the forum, is "How do you deal with them when they continue to assert that they will only negotiate a peace treaty as a nuclear power?" They assert that because they are a nuclear power, they want to negotiate as a nuclear power. Unless you secure some type of a reference from them, disingenuous though it may be, that they are willing to abide by that commitment, you validate their claim to nuclear status. It's a very difficult diplomatic conundrum, because, while you can have talks about talks; and you can exercise diplomacy, which, again, about which I think we saw the previous panel refer to the efficacy and the necessity of; but, in terms of formal negotiations, there is a Catch 22 there, based on North Korea's standing position, that we have to address.

Dr. NOLAND. I would say that of course we have to talk to them bilaterally, if only to do the sorts of testing that you were raising with the previous panel.

But, I would just align myself with Mr. Flakes' statement. The real key to the six-party talks is not the talks themselves, which appear to be somewhat awkward, but it's that September 2005 statement. That's the one thing we have that puts the North Koreans on the hook for denuclearization. And that would seem to be a big thing to throw away.

The CHAIRMAN. I think that's smart. I think you don't want to throw it away, but that doesn't mean you need to tie yourself, as a methodology for getting forward, to that particular structure, which I think is cumbersome, and which I think, if you go back to its first days, was really put together more as a mechanism, not really for having the talks, but for handling certain politics. And I think we've been tied down by that.

Mr. Carlin, I have additional questions I wanted to ask you. I'd like to follow up. But, unfortunately, I have a meeting coming up in a moment, and I've used up my time. And Senator Lugar also has a thing. So, if we could—we're going to leave the record open, as I said, and I'd like to get back to you, if I can, to follow up on this a little bit, even since we're a little time-pressed here today, if that's OK with you.

But, I really appreciate it. I thought all of your comments were very perceptive. Your statements underscore, to some degree, problems with our—the driving perceptions of how we've been thinking about this. And I think we've got to really step back and not deal with mythology or with a stereotype of what the give-and-take is here. And I think your warnings are very appropriate and helpful in that regard.

So, I thank you for coming in today. This will not be our last conversation about this. And I appreciate your willingness to share your thoughts and expertise with the committee today. It's very helpful.

Senator Lugar, if you could——

Senator LUGAR. May I——

The CHAIRMAN [continuing]. Close things out.

Senator LUGAR [continuing]. Conclude the hearing by asking——

The CHAIRMAN. Yes.

Senator LUGAR [continuing]. A few more questions?

The CHAIRMAN. No, no, no, that's absolutely your hearing.

Thank you.

Senator LUGAR [presiding]. Thanks very much.

Now, I'm curious—because I think both you, Dr. Noland, and Mr. Carlin, have mentioned that at least some persons in North Korea have access to information from the outside world, press accounts of some sort—but, I'm curious what information you have about access to the Internet and social media. To what extent are either the young people, the middle-aged, or anyone in North Korea, on the Internet or, beyond that, using social networking Web sites such as Twitter or what have you? Is this something that's just simply not arrived in North Korea, or are the people who have this access so embedded in the regime that we're not seeing the same results that we're seeing in other regimes that have had some problems with this?

Dr. NOLAND. The North Korean approach to these issues is characteristic of highly authoritarian regimes. On the one hand, there is a desire to show that they're a technologically advanced society. On the other hand, there's an extreme concern about the implications of these kinds of ways of communicating.

So, what the North Koreans have effectively done is, they've created their own internal Internet. So, you have an Internet that lots of people, at least in urban areas, can get on to, but it's only within North Korea. Literally the number of cables going out of the country that allow one to make international calls or data transmissions is very limited. So, the number of people who have access to the Internet, as we would understand it, is a very small group of the elite, the people that Mr. Carlin normally interacts with. There is some ability, in the northern border areas, to use cell telephones that work off the Chinese system. And presumably, a greater degree of information can pass through that channel than through the cellular system within the country.

On the one hand, there's a desire to show they're an advanced country and that they have lots of technology. But, on the other hand, there is also a very profound desire to control the potential political implications of that technology.

Senator LUGAR. Mr. Carlin, do you have a comment on this?

Mr. CARLIN. Well, it's worth noting that the number of cell phones in the country has increased significantly in the last few years. This cell phone infrastructure has been improved and built so that something like 70 or 80 percent of the country is now covered, in terms of cell phone towers. And the number of young people that they're training on how to use computers, and how to sort of become computer literate at least, is really quite remarkable, so that when and if this access ever is opened up to the international-based Internet, I believe it's going to spread rather quickly. And, in fact, if I were a North Korean Ministry of Security officer, I'd be very nervous, at this point, at what I see happening in this society.

Senator LUGAR. To what extent can we help accelerate this access through our broadcasts? You know, we've had hearings with regard to our broadcasting mechanisms to China, for example, as well as to other Asian countries, which have been extremely interesting. And you've mentioned at least some ties with China and the cell phone business. I'm just curious, along purely the information line, the broadcasting line, what possibilities do we have utilizing that, quite apart from the economic sanctions or the punishment routes that we have employed?

Dr. NOLAND. Well, right now we have Radio Free Asia, which broadcasts into North Korea——

Senator LUGAR. Yes.

Dr. NOLAND [continuing]. A Korean-language broadcast, but they're on a shortwave and they're broadcast from transmitters that are quite far away.

There are three things we could do to improve the effectiveness. No. 1, increase the number of hours of programming. No. 2, move to a.m. And No. 3, try to convince some of our allies to allow the stationing of transmitters in their countries, which would allow much more effective transmission.

Senator LUGAR. It would not appear to me that we have been particularly aggressive in our own policies or our own organization of this, but do you have any comments about that?

Yes, Mr. Flake.

Mr. FLAKE. I would just note that, here again, the real game is inter-Korean. There is a very active civil society in Korea operating both out of the borderlands on the Chinese border, but also out of South Korea itself, which is specifically strategizing about how to get information, in Korean, into North Korea. Obviously, again, per the media reports in the last few days, this is something that's of great concern to the North Korean leadership.

Another interesting, kind of, factoid in this regard: The cell phone provider in North Korea is Orascom, an Egyptian company with close ties between Kim Jong-il and, of course, Hosni Mubarak. As such, it will be very interesting to see how things play out with that particular contract in the weeks to come.

There are, by my understanding, some 260,000 to maybe 300,000 cell phones in operation in North Korea right now; the vast majority within Pyongyang, itself, and among the elite. But, that said, such phones are an information transmission vehicle that did not exist before, particularly among the elite, who are the most likely to be disillusioned, in terms of recognizing the difference between expectations and reality.

This is a very important factor, in terms of understanding where North Korea's likely to go in the near future.

Senator LUGAR. Let me follow through on a comment that one of you made, that there may be 20,000 North Koreans in South Korea as refugees. In some past hearings we've heard that, by and large, the South Koreans have not been particularly receptive of people coming from North Korea. This may be a broad generalization, but we perceived that South Koreans were by and large in favor of unity in due course, but, at the same time, that they had a desire to absorb only a few persons at a time in order to avoid, in their view, inheriting all of the problems of North Korea. On the other hand, given that now the disparity in terms of wealth and economics between the two Koreas is so great, why wouldn't the South Koreans as a matter of policy, welcome more refugees from North Korea in order to build more of a population that, in terms of either communication or an interpretation of what's occurring, would be helpful to South Korea?

Mr. FLAKE. I'll start off with that, and the others can chime in, as well.

There has been a remarkable shift, in terms of how South Korea views refugees or defectors coming out of North Korea, that is commensurate with the shift in the Government in South Korea. During 10 years of progressive governments in Seoul, the national narrative was all about cooperation, working with North Korea. And so, defectors, particularly those with horrendous human rights stories, coming over, kind of, didn't fit well——

Senator LUGAR. Yes.

Mr. FLAKE [continuing]. Within that narrative, and they didn't feel welcome, on a policy level. Obviously, there are still deep problems of social integration for North Korean refugees integrating into South Korean society. For the bulk of the 50-some-odd years of national separation, the flow of defectors was so small that South Korea could afford to give them large sums of money, stipends to keep them living and educate them and get them jobs, et cetera. In the last several years, that number has continued to grow and this is becoming in some respects, an immigration issue with all the budget consequences that are related to that, as well.

But, that said, I would think that, at least in my mind, compared to 3 years ago the environment right now is much improved and continues to be so depending on the level of flow.

Dr. NOLAND. As Mr. Flake said, there are problems with integration and assimilation, and one shouldn't underestimate the traumas that these people have experienced. In our refugee interviews, I would say that probably half the people we interviewed, in a clinical setting, would be diagnosed with post-traumatic stress disorder; the famine, incarceration in the penal system, have profound psychological impact. So, it's a traumatized population. And there is increasing understanding of this in South Korea. The South Korean Government has passed new legislation, which is, I think, really improving the quality of services that it's providing to these people. And, I think that there is hope that this population will be better served, moving forward, than it perhaps has been in the past.

Senator LUGAR. Mr. Carlin, I'd like to ask, from your very vast knowledge of the internal workings of North Korea: What are the specific steps, if we were to have a bilateral talk or talks with North Korea, that would advance the denuclearization situation?

Mr. CARLIN. I'm afraid that—well, I would say, the steps that we would take to advance denuclearization are not to talk about it right away, quite frankly. I think the situation has so deteriorated, in terms of our own position, that it would not be a wise strategy to start off with that subject, because we won't get anywhere and the negative result will poison the entire process.

I think if, now, we want to get to denuclearization, it's going to take us longer than it would have before. And we're going to have to explore a broader horizon with the North Koreans, in an effort to establish some sort of common ground from which to speak to each other, and then eventually zero in on that, since it is so important to us.

Senator LUGAR. Well, one of the reasons often given for the six-power talks is that they include Japan. And from time to time, over, now, a couple of decades, quite apart from the last few years, the Japanese, broadly, have indicated that they did not pursue nuclear weapons because they had confidence in the United States and our ability to work with them for their protection. This was shaken, on occasion, when North Korea apparently fired missiles that straddled Japan, or in some geographical formation. And they came to us with considerable anxiety, asking "Where were you? And how can we count on you?" and so forth.

Maybe the other powers involved, particularly Japan, perhaps the South Koreans, have some problems with this degree of patience. But, your feeling still is, given the regime problems, the potential changes, and so forth, that there just are not persons presently in North Korea that are prepared if the United States asked, today, if we could sit down to get to that issue, except after a good number of intervening steps and other issues.

Mr. CARLIN. I'm afraid that every lesson that we've taught to the North Koreans over the last 10 years is that they'd be much better served by relying on a nuclear deterrent than on our good word. And we have to teach them the opposite now. And it's going to take us a while to do that. We're going to have to follow through on agreements, as will they. I'm not suggesting this is one-sided. But, we have a lot of homework to do and a lot of brambles to clear in the path ahead of us, because of some policies that we've followed in the past.

I would say it ill behooves the Japanese to worry about the pacing of our talks with the North Koreans, when they are so focused on a single domestic issue, which they consider quite important—it's quite emotional; no one can second-guess them on it. But, the fact is, they're so fixated on that, that they're not being very helpful to us in our own attempts to deal with this larger regional problem.

Senator LUGAR. What if—I would ask of any of you—a situation occurs in which the regime succession does not work out quite in the pattern that has been prescribed, and, in fact, just to use a cliche, a military government of some sort succeeds this family situation? What is your prediction as to how whatever leadership may arise in that form would deal with the problems we've been talking about? Is it simply more of the same? Are there any indications that, as a matter of fact, such a government would have a different outlook toward South Koreans, toward the Chinese, toward us, toward nuclear issues?

Mr. CARLIN. To the extent that, as I think is true, that North Koreans, at least at the level you're talking about, really do see themselves as part of a legitimate country with legitimate interests, I think we're fooling ourselves to think that, when the family is replaced, that suddenly, you know, Hosanna, they'll have a—they'll see the world as we do, especially against the South Koreans. So, I wouldn't necessarily look forward to that sort of a shift in regimes. I wouldn't think, off the top of my head, that it would make the situation better for us. Whether it's more dangerous or not would—might depend a lot on the personalities involved.

Senator LUGAR. Yes, sir. Mr. Flake.

Mr. FLAKE. I would very much agree with Mr. Carlin. It is difficult to imagine almost any scenario where known factions in North Korea taking over would make things better. If anything, the instability and everything associated with that, would probably make things worse, going forward.

That said, I'd like to take just a moment to talk about the broader question that he was addressing, in terms of how you move forward in facing that fundamental challenge of: "How do we deal with a North Korea that has declared itself a nuclear power?" I think the plan that Mr. Carlin outlined makes perfect sense if you're looking at North Korea in a vacuum. I mean, what he has described to you is exactly what we would need to do if we were to get North Korea, themselves, to decide that they eventually wanted to give up the nuclear weapons.

But, unfortunately, as you rightly pointed out, Mr. Senator, that we're not dealing with North Korea in a vacuum. You've got a lot of other countries in the immediate region, and the world writ large, that are looking very closely at the lessons we are drawing from North Korea. And, at this point, North Korea is the only country ever to have pulled out of the NPT and the IAEA. And, if a country of North Korea's status and demonstrated past behavior, as the previous panel talked about in quite great detail, talking about nonproliferation—if a country with a demonstrated past of proliferation, of selling any weapon system it can get its hands on, with all the human rights and other issues we've discussed here—if they can become recognized as a nuclear power, even a de facto recognized as a nuclear power, who can't? What country in the world today is not more acceptable to the international community as a nuclear power than North Korea?

So, unfortunately, this is—while absolutely agreeing with Mr. Carlin that this is what the North Korean leaders may want, I think that the reality that the government today is faced with, and that future governments will be faced with, is that it's extremely challenging to move forward with North Korea because of their statements and their nuclear tests. We are in a very different stage of these negotiations than we were maybe 15 or 20 years ago.

Senator LUGAR. Finally, I'll——

Dr. NOLAND. If I could——

Senator LUGAR. Yes, Dr. Noland.

Dr. NOLAND. I think it's very difficult, or if not impossible, to predict what some successor leadership might want to do. I think what we probably can say is that there won't be major changes while Kim Jong-il is still alive. The problem, of course, is that this is a political culture that creates enormous incentives for people to falsify their true preferences. And when the situation changes, it may be possible for individuals or factions to develop that actually take the country in a somewhat different direction. I mean, it's not impossible to imagine that some successor leadership would look around at the wreckage and kind of decide there must be some better way of doing things.

That said, even if such a faction were to come to power and want to pursue some sorts of reforms, either internally or in their external relations, doing so would not necessarily be easy. The divided nature of the Peninsula creates a fundamental legitimacy challenge for the North Korean regime. And once they start moving closer to South Korea and looking more like South Korea, then the whole justification for the maintenance of North Korea as an independent state could be called into question. So, I don't think that we can rule out the possibility of a more enlightened leadership in the future, but I don't think we can count on it, and I don't think we can underestimate the difficulty that such a leadership might face in trying to take the country in a different direction.

Senator LUGAR. Well, my final question is: In the event of some change, despite its cause, to what extent are extensive Chinese investments in North Korea—we've already suggested there may be some extensive South Korean investments—but, to what extent would either party attempt to pursue protection of its interests? Or are they large enough, in relationship to their respective economies, to make that much of a difference? Do people just simply take their losses and assume that this was the luck of the draw?

Dr. NOLAND. I think that we can assume that there is a rivalry between China and South Korea for economic influence in North Korea, and that that would play into the behavior of both of those governments. However, at least from a kind of mathematical standpoint, if you look at the North Korean economy today, and you look at the size of those investments, in any kind of macroeconomic sense or broader sense, in terms of either the Chinese or the South Korean Governments, these investments are trivial. This is a country in which the investments that will be needed to rehabilitate that economy are vast, relative to the foreign investments that exist there today.

Senator LUGAR. Well, I thank each one of you very much for your statements, that are a part of the record, and for your remarkable testimony and your response to our questions. I believe this has been a very productive hearing, and you have certainly helped make that the case.

Let me make a final statement. I ask consent that a letter written by Ambassador Charles "Jack" Pritchard, longtime East Asia expert and current president of the Korean Economic Institute, to myself and Senator Kerry in preparation for this hearing, be submitted for the record.

Senator LUGAR. And the record will remain open for QFRs until the close of business on Friday, March the 4th.

And I would add that, in addition to this report, a short opinion piece, likewise, be included in the record.

And, at least, since no one is going to object——

[Laughter.]

Senator LUGAR [continuing]. I declare that this will be in the record, to complete that record with our QFRs to be submitted until March 4.

Senator LUGAR. Thank you so very much. We appreciate your coming.

And the hearing is adjourned.

[Whereupon, at 12:32 p.m., the hearing was adjourned.]

---

## ADDITIONAL MATERIAL SUBMITTED FOR THE RECORD

### PREPARED STATEMENT OF HON. MICHAEL S. LEE, U.S. SENATOR FROM UTAH

Thank you Assistant Secretary Campbell, Representative Bosworth, Mr. Carlin and Mr. Noland for your participation in this hearing.

Thank you, Senators Kerry and Lugar for your leadership in discussing the volatile situation in North Korea. While events in Egypt and Libya have commanded our attention over the past weeks and months, circumstances in North Korea demand our vigilance and preparation to ensure the safety and security of the United States and our allies in Asia.

---

### LETTER AND N.Y. OP-ED SUBMITTED BY AMBASSADOR CHARLES "JACK" PRITCHARD

KOREA ECONOMIC INSTITUTE,
*Washington, DC, February 25, 2011.*

Re Senate Foreign Relations Committee Hearing on "Breaking the Cycle of North Korean Provocations"

Hon. JOHN F. KERRY,
*Chairman, U.S. Senate Committee On Foreign Relations,*
*U.S. Senate, Washington, DC.*

Hon. Richard G. Lugar,
*Ranking Member, U.S. Senate Committee On Foreign Relations,*
*U.S. Senate, Washington, DC.*

DEAR CHAIRMAN KERRY AND SENATOR LUGAR: It is with deep appreciation of the Committee's work on U.S. policy toward North Korea that I offer a few observations in advance of the March 1, 2011 hearing on "Breaking the Cycle of North Korean Provocations."

With regard to breaking the cycle of provocations, 1 believe that the worst-case military provocations that we witnessed in 2010 will not be repeated except in extraordinary circumstances. In 2010, we witnessed unacceptable North Korean provocative behavior: the sinking of the *Cheonan* in March and the shelling of Yeonpyeong Island in November. The first caused the deaths of 46 sailors; in the latter case, 4 were killed. I also think it is important to try to understand why 2010 was such a bad year when it comes to North Korea's unacceptable behavior.

For North Korea, 2010 was a critical year. Kim Jong-il was still recovering from his stroke in August 2008; the succession process was high on their agenda; sanctions were creating difficulties; currency revaluation had gone terribly wrong; and the North Koreans harbored thoughts of revenge for the November 2009 West Sea incident that humiliated the military.

On the international front, Pyongyang had a lot going against it; intra-Korean relations were at a low point and the United States was steadfastly ignoring its calls for bilateral engagement. In other words, there was nothing positive going on to moderate Pyongyang's worst tendencies. Domestically, Pyongyang needed a reason to rally the nation around Kim Jong-il and his eventual successor. The easiest way to do that was through the military.

I believe North Korea was prepared to react violently to any perceived provocation or slight. They chose to take action around the Northern Limit Line in the West Sea. As they thought through the consequences, they determined that South Korea was unlikely to respond in an overly aggressive manner and if they were successful, the increased tensions would work in Kim's favor. After both the *Cheonan* and Yeonpyeong incidents, we heard stories fabricated to embellish Kim Jong-un's credibility within the military—key to his ultimate successful succession to power.

And unfortunately, they correctly calculated that China would not do anything that would substantially harm Pyongyang's interests.

So what does the current charm offensive by Pyongyang mean, particularly when you think how quickly they have reversed course. They went from attacking South Korea militarily to offering dialogue at anytime, at anywhere and criticizing Seoul for not jumping at the opportunity.

I think it is consistent with Pyongyang's 2 main objectives. First and foremost is the need to reduce external tension in 2011 in the run up to 2012—the 100th anniversary of Kim Il-Sung's birth. As you know, North Korea has declared that it will be a strong and prosperous nation in 2012. In order to do that, it needs foreign direct investment and opportunities to create hard currency. The international community's adverse reaction to the activities of 2010 proved that aggressive behavior will not lead to achieving this goal.

Secondly, I believe enough overt attention has been given Kim Jong-un; protective measures have been put in place to ensure the survival of the Kim family after Kim Jong-il's death; and Kim Jong-un's legend is off to a strong start—certainly in the minds of the North Korean leadership. Any additional emphasis on Kim Jong-un now comes at the direct expense of Kim Jong-il. He may be thinking of his eventual demise, but he does not want to become irrelevant before his death. In this regard, 2011 should be far less confrontational than 2010.

Additionally, I have attached a copy of a recently submitted op-ed (to the NY Times) in which I propose a specific, comprehensive, proactive U.S. policy toward North Korea. I hope these thoughts will be of use in preparation for your upcoming hearing.

Sincerely,

Ambassador CHARLES L. (JACK) PRITCHARD,
*President, Korea Economic Institute.*

ATTACHMENT

NY TIMES OP-ED OF JACK PRITCHARD, PRESIDENT OF THE KOREA ECONOMIC INSTITUTE

Last year I was privileged to co-chair the Council on Foreign Relations Independent Task Force Report, "U.S. Policy Toward the Korean Peninsula." The Task Force was made up, as all CFR Task Forces, of a prestigious group of experts who found that the "Obama administration's current approach does not go far enough in developing a strategy to counter North Korea's continuing nuclear development or potential for proliferation." The Task Force made several recommendations that the administration has yet to implement.

One of the Task Force's observation was that there was "significant risk that (the administration's ) 'strategic patience' will result in acquiescence to North Korea's nuclear status as a fait accompli." Several months have transpired since the report was published in June 2010 and "strategic patience" continues even in the wake of the sinking of the South Korean naval vessel *Cheonan* and the artillery shelling of the South Korean island which combined killed 50 South Koreans.

That is not to imply that U.S. policy should change in reaction to bad behavior by North Korea, but rather it is meant to suggest that the lack of a policy (or at best a passive policy) is not sufficient to prevent proliferation or move us closer to denuclearization. Meanwhile North Korean provocations have increased tension on the peninsula.

The emphasis the administration places on its solidarity with Seoul and its insistence that Pyongyang first improve relations with South Korea along with its "at arms' length" approach to North Korea served an initial useful purpose. It changed the dynamic of past administrations' knee jerk-like reaction to Pyongyang's every move. It was healthy to reset the ground rules under which an American administration would engage North Korea. However, there is a point when this approach begins to be counterproductive to the ultimate goal of denuclearization and non-proliferation. We have long since reached that point.

Certainly, the administration should continue close consultations with Seoul. The benefit to the alliance as a whole has been remarkable, but it is time for the administration to put forth a proactive North Korea policy.

Washington and Seoul have told Pyongyang that it must demonstrate sincerity before they are willing to reengage in Six-Party Talks designed to achieve denuclearization of the Korean Peninsula. For its part, North Korea has been clear in its message that it is willing to return to talks (under gentle pressure from Beijing), but that the agenda should be refocused on the "root cause" of the nuclear problem—U.S. hostility towards Pyongyang. Because of the Kim regime's narrow focus on promoting nationalism in support of the eventual succession of power to a third generation Kim, actual denuclearization is off the table. This is a formula for continued stalemate.

If U.S. policy remains on the current course, there is little potential that our security concerns will be resolved and every chance that North Korea will drift toward de facto nuclear weapons state status.

This calls for a comprehensive, proactive policy toward North Korea. This is best done by articulating an objective of absolute denuclearization of North Korea using the robust application of United Nations Security Council Resolution 1874 as a means of shaping Pyongyang's security environment. That requires continuous engagement with Beijing to ensure that it does not deviate from our common objective and that China willingly applies reasonable and sufficient leverage on Pyongyang to ensure North Korea does not believe that there is a viable Chinese loophole in UNSC sanctions.

Reengaging North Korea in a multilateral forum (Six-Party Talks) will be of limited value as long as Pyongyang is overly concerned about the long-term survivability of its regime. Its nuclear weapons program is the equivalent of a night light. Take it away and they are not sure they will survive the night.

Once the basics are in place, the United States needs to actively engage North Korea on a host of issues for which we and they have concerns. These issues roughly fall into the following broad categories: humanitarian, security, confidence building, and economic.

Specifically, Washington should open up a distinct dialogue on medical requirements such as tuberculosis management and family reunions between Korean-Americans and North Korean relatives separated by the Korean War. A discussion on best agricultural practices along with sponsorship of student educational opportunities would go a long way in addressing chronic North Korean problems associated with its self-imposed isolation and contribute to the promotion of positive external influences. A corollary discussion on disaster prevention and the development of a regional response package led by the Red Cross would assist in minimizing the impact natural and man-made disasters have on the welfare of the North Korean people.

Engaging Pyongyang on its long-range missile program will not be easy. More than ten years have elapsed since the last serious discussion on this critical issue was held. At one point, a self-imposed missile moratorium held North Korea's missile development and proliferation ambitions in check. Pyongyang has used the desire to orbit a satellite as a rationale for its recent missile tests. A permutation of an idea that may have originated in a Putin-Kim Jong il meeting in the summer of 2000 in which other countries would take on the delivery of North Korean satellites in exchange for a permanent moratorium on its testing and fielding of long-range missiles needs to be re-examined as a potential starting point.

Likewise, the nuclear fuel cycle discussion that is gaining ground elsewhere needs to be imported into a North Korean context. However much the administration currently believes Pyongyang has violated Security Council sanctions and inter-Korean agreements, it does not change basic facts. North Korea is building an experimental light water reactor which, if they are successful, could lead to larger, full scale reactors which would rely on the fuel from the recently revealed uranium enrichment facility. The administration may want to apply a new set of sanctions for North Korea's entry into the fuel cycle business, but it is not likely to happen (as we have seen from China's recent blockage of a U.N. report on Pyongyang's uranium facility) and at the end of the day we will be where we are now: suspecting that North Korea has a secret highly enriched uranium facility capable of producing bomb-grade enriched uranium and hoping that the claimed low enriched uranium facility does not morph into a nuclear weapons related facility. Bringing North Korea into the fuel cycle dialogue is the best way to guard against this latter concern and perhaps open the door to discussing Pyongyang's highly enriched uranium program.

With regard to confidence building, we should begin a preliminary four party dialogue involving North Korea, China, South Korea and the United States on replacing the current armistice for a more permanent peace arrangement. The precedent for this was the original four party peace talks more than a decade ago that had just such a goal. The primary benefit of the discussion would be to lay the groundwork on what both the south and north require before moving at an appropriate time and venue to negotiate an actual peace treaty. The lead role played by Seoul and Pyongyang would support the administration's desire for improved North-South relations and enhance the near-term benefit of identifying and implementing confidence building measures short of a peace treaty that would inevitably reduce tension on the peninsula.

On the economic front, a serious energy survey of North Korea's energy capacity is a necessary starting point to establish what types of energy assistance other parties could provide should there ever be the kind of progress in denuclearization talks that warranted assistance. The precedence and promise of energy assistance is well established. What is lacking is a current forum to ensure the best empirical data is available for parties to make the right choices.

In anticipation of eventual success in denuclearizing North Korea and as a tangible incentive to Pyongyang, a dialogue on practical foreign direct investments in North Korea needs to get underway. Sectors for promising joint ventures need to be identified, rules clarified, and limits understood.

In all, there are over ten specific areas where we can begin work with North Korea that reinforces the positive and gives Pyongyang the impetus for seriously weighing the advantages for making the decision to get rid of its nuclear weapons program. As long as the basic framework of full application of UNSCR 1874 is in force, this approach would not run the risk of creating non-humanitarian safety valves which would unduly delay Pyongyang's ultimate decision to eliminate its nuclear weapons program.

————

RESPONSES OF SPECIAL REPRESENTATIVE STEPHEN BOSWORTH TO QUESTIONS SUBMITTED BY SENATOR JOHN F. KERRY

*Question.* How likely is it that the North Korean Government will collapse in the next 3–5 years? If the Kim Jong-il regime falters, do you believe a new government will be more or less willing to abandon the pursuit of nuclear weapons?

*Answer.* We are carefully watching developments in Pyongyang. North Korea is one of the world's most closed societies, so it is difficult to predict the future composition of the North Korean regime or its policies.

*Question.* Do you believe U.S. diplomatic engagement with North Korea makes economic reform and political reform more or less likely?

*Answer.* The United States remains open to diplomatically engaging North Korea on denuclearization, but this process and its outcomes depend on the decisions and actions of North Korea. If North Korea improves relations with South Korea and demonstrates a change in behavior, including taking irreversible steps to denuclearize, complying with international law, and ceasing provocative behavior, it can achieve security, economic opportunity, and respect from the international community. However, if it continues on its pattern of confrontation and isolation and fails to comply with its obligations and commitments, it stands no chance of becoming a strong and prosperous nation.

*Question.* Are North Korean provocations—nuclear tests, missile tests, proliferation of nuclear and missile technology, and demilitarized zone violations—more or less likely in the absence of high-level U.S. diplomatic engagement?

*Answer.* We have maintained high-level engagement on this issue. When North Korea sank the ROK naval vessel *Cheonan* in March 2010, the United States had been seeking to resume serious negotiations on denuclearization, as evidenced by my December 2009 trip to Pyongyang. Following the DPRK's sinking of the *Cheonan,* disclosure of a uranium enrichment program (UEP), and shelling of Yeonpyong Island, we have continued to engage in intensive diplomatic activities building consensus among our allies and Five-Party partners that the DPRK's provocations are unacceptable and will not be rewarded.

Our diplomatic response has included the dispatch of several high-level delegations to the region. Moreover, during a historic December 7 trilateral ministerial, the United States, ROK, and Japan declared that the DPRK's provocative and belligerent behavior threatens all three countries and will be met with solidarity from all three countries. We have also continually consulted with China on how it can best use its influence with North Korea. During Chinese President Hu's January 2011visit to Washington, the two sides issued a United States-China Joint Statement which "expressed concern regarding the DPRK's claimed uranium enrichment program," "opposed all activities inconsistent with the 2005 Joint Statement and relevant international obligations and commitments," and "called for the necessary steps that would allow for the early resumption of the six-party talks process to address this and other relevant issues." In addition to fostering unprecedented Five-Party coordination, these diplomatic efforts have preserved regional stability.

*Question.* Looking ahead, is it possible to set the terms of our diplomatic engagement in ways that will not reward North Korea's bad behavior?

*Answer.* We have made it clear that we are open to diplomatically engaging North Korea on denuclearization. However, this process depends on the decisions and actions of North Korea. We are looking for evidence that North Korea is not only seriously committed to negotiations but also that such negotiations could be constructive. We are working very closely with our Five-Party partners to identify a path that we believe will lead to constructive engagement with the DPRK. We have made clear that a path would be open if the DPRK took steps to improve North-

South relations and demonstrated a change in behavior, including taking actions toward irreversible denuclearization; complying with international law, including its commitments under the 2005 Joint Statement of the Six-Party Talks and its obligations under U.N. Security Council Resolutions 1718 and 1874; and ceasing provocative behavior.

*Question.* The September 19, 2005, Six Party Talks Joint Statement contained six provisions reflecting overlapping mutual obligations. The core pledges included the following:

- North Korea pledged to abandon all nuclear weapons and existing nuclear programs and return, at an early date, to the Treaty on the Non-Proliferation of Nuclear Weapons and to safeguards established by the International Atomic Energy Agency;
- The United States affirmed that it has no nuclear weapons on the Korean Peninsula and has no intention to attack or invade North Korea with nuclear or conventional weapons.
- The United States and the other parties also agreed to discuss, at an appropriate time, the subject of the provision of a light water reactor to North Korea.
- North Korea and the United States undertook to respect each other's sovereignty, exist peacefully together, and take steps to normalize their relations subject to their respective bilateral policies.
- China, Japan, South Korea, Russia and the United States stated their willingness to provide energy assistance to North Korea.

If the DPRK abides by all of its pledges, does the United States remain willing to fulfill all of its commitments under the September 19, 2005, Joint Statement? If not, which pledges does the United States intend to renegotiate in light of the changed circumstances on the Korean Peninsula (such as the North's nuclear and missile tests, its reported sensitive proliferation activities, its violations of the armistice, and its independent pursuit of light water nuclear reactor technology)?

*Answer.* If the DPRK fulfills its commitments under the 2005 Joint Statement of the Six-Party Talks, including abandoning all nuclear weapons and existing nuclear programs and returning, at an early date, to the Treaty on the Non-Proliferation of Nuclear Weapons and to International Atomic Energy Agency safeguards, the United States remains willing to fulfill all of its joint statement commitments.

*Question.* The stated goal of U.S. policy remains accomplishing the complete, verifiable, and irreversible denuclearization of the Korean Peninsula.

- Is there a benefit to establishing manageable benchmarks toward this final objective? Are there interim goals such as verifiably capping fissile material production, securing a moratorium on nuclear and missile tests, and receiving assurances on proliferation, for which the United States would be willing to provide incentives and/or some sanctions relief?

*Answer.* The United States seeks the verifiable denuclearization of the Korean Peninsula in a peaceful manner. However, verifiable capping of fissile material production, securing a moratorium on nuclear and missile tests, and receiving assurances on proliferation are among the intermediate goals we are also pursuing in order to achieve the ultimate objective.

*Question.* We know other countries, including Iran, are likely watching events on the Korean Peninsula with considerable interest. Is the above approach, which acknowledges the potential realities of the situation, consistent with our global non-proliferation agenda?

*Answer.* Our approaches to nonproliferation challenges may vary depending on the circumstances of each case, but our objectives are consistent: to uphold and strengthen the nonproliferation regime and to prevent and eliminate threats to international security caused by the spread of nuclear weapons and proliferation-sensitive technologies. In that regard, we expect North Korea to take irreversible steps toward denuclearization, to return to the Nuclear Non-Proliferation Treaty and International Atomic Energy Agency (IAEA) safeguards, and to comply with its U.N. Security Council Resolution (UNSCR) obligations. In cases where the IAEA Board of Governors or the U.N. Security Council has required action, we expect states to comply with those obligations as well. We have also actively urged all states to implement UNSCRs 1718 and 1874 fully and transparently to prevent proliferation to and from the DPRK.

*Question.* The United States Government has historically supported a broad range of humanitarian outreach to the DPRK, including food aid, assistance on public health (such as tuberculosis control), POW–MIA recovery operations, people-to-people initiatives, cultural and educational exchanges, and even limited technical outreach to bureaucrats. But over the past few years, such efforts have been suspended.

- What is the administration's position on broadening and deepening our humanitarian engagement with the DPRK? Does humanitarian outreach help promote gradual changes inside North Korea that are advantageous in terms of U.S. interests?

Answer. Our humanitarian assistance is not linked to any political or security issues.The United States remains concerned about the well-being of the North Korean people. The U.S. Government's policy on the provision of humanitarian assistance is based on three factors: (1) the level of need in a given country; (2) competing needs in other countries; and (3) our ability to ensure that aid is reliably reaching the people in need. This policy is consistent with our longstanding goal of providing emergency humanitarian assistance to the people of countries around the world where there are legitimate humanitarian needs. However, consistent with our practice worldwide, the United States will not provide food aid without a needs assessment and adequate program management, monitoring, and access provisions in place.

*Question.* As a matter of policy, does the administration link food aid and medical assistance to nonhumanitarian considerations?

Answer. The U.S. Government does not link food aid and medical assistance to nonhumanitarian considerations. Our longstanding goal is to provide emergency humanitarian assistance to the people of countries around the world where there are legitimate humanitarian needs.

*Question.* What is the Obama administration's policy on the issuance of visas to North Koreans interested in participating in humanitarian, cultural, or scientific exchanges?

Answer. The United States believes that exchanges can help develop technical knowledge in critical areas such as agriculture, energy, and medicine, as well as encourage greater awareness of the outside world by North Koreans. We look forward to North Korea taking actions that will allow for the expansion of educational, cultural, and people-to-people exchange programs.

*Question.* What impact has (i) rising global food prices; (ii) the rising price of international crude oil; (iii) recent flooding and droughts in North Korea; and (iv) the North Korean attempt at currency reform had on the food situation in North Korea?

Answer. The North Korean Government's unwise economic policies, including its failed attempt at currency reform in late 2009, are the primary causes of the country's weakened food security situation. Rising global food prices, the rising price of international crude oil, and recent flooding and droughts in North Korea have only served to exacerbate a situation resulting from the regime's poor choices. The 2010 DPRK Human Rights Report notes that food shortages initially followed the currency reform. Chronic shortages in food supplies could be addressed by the DPRK if the North Korean Government implemented appropriate economic policies encouraging private sector-led growth and development.

In the near term, rising global food prices are expected to further reduce the North Korean Government's ability to import food to meet the projected gap between food production and food needs in 2011. The impact of the rising price of international crude oil, while difficult to quantify, could also inhibit the purchase of essential agricultural inputs and add costs to the North Korean Government's dispersal of food through the Public Distribution System.

*Question.* From February 8–15, 2011, a rapid food security assessment was completed in three North Korean provinces by a needs assessment team that included five nongovernmental organizations (NGOs): Christian Friends of Korea, Global Resource Services, Mercy Corps, Samaritan's Purse, and World Vision. What were the principle findings of this NGO delegation?

Answer. The visit was requested by the North Korean Government, whose representatives informed the aid NGOs of claimed food shortages in North Korea. The United States did not ask the five aid agencies to conduct their recent food assessment nor act on behalf of the U.S. Government. The United States continues to be concerned for the well-being of the North Korean people.

According to their press release, the five aid agencies found evidence of looming food shortages and acute malnutrition in the DPRK. The seven-member team traveled to the provinces of North Pyongan, South Pyongan, and Chagang from February 8–15. We understand that the team visited 45 sites including hospitals, orphanages, citizens' homes, cooperative farms and warehouses. We also understand that the team that observed some evidence of malnutrition and food shortages, which were particularly prevalent among families that depend on the North Korean public food distribution system and most severely impact children, the elderly, the chronically ill, and pregnant and nursing mothers.

*Question.* What is the Obama administration's assessment of the monitoring and verification of food assistance that occurred during the 2008–09 period? As part of your answer, please evaluate the adequacy of safeguards that were in place to prevent diversion of food assistance.

Answer. The United States remains concerned about the well-being of the North Korean people. Our last food assistance program was abruptly suspended by the North Koreans in March 2009, and our humanitarian personnel were ordered to leave the country and forced to leave behind over 20,000 metric tons of U.S. food items. The question of what happened to the unmonitored aid is a key concern that must be addressed before any discussion of providing future food aid is begun.

Consistent with our practices worldwide, the United States will not provide food aid without a thorough needs assessment and adequate program management, monitoring, and access provisions in place. Before the start of the 2008–09 program, we negotiated the strongest monitoring and verification safeguards in the history of international humanitarian assistance programs in North Korea. These standards have not been met since the program ended.

*Question.* Have North Korean officials made any representations within the past year to their U.S. counterparts on adherence to monitoring and verification arrangements for food assistance?

Answer. The United States works on this matter through diplomatic channels. The details of our diplomatic conversations can be shared in a classified setting.

*Question.* If there is a demonstrated need, if the United States determines that the situation ranks serious enough compared to other humanitarian crises, and if North Korea is willing to accede to robust verification and monitoring arrangements to ensure that food is distributed to those most in need, would the administration support the resumption of food aid to North Korea?

Answer. The U.S. Government assesses that the DPRK suffers from a chronic food shortage. We remain deeply concerned about the well-being of the North Korean people, however, consistent with our practices worldwide, U.S. food aid is contingent on a thorough needs assessment as well as competing international needs and adequate program management, monitoring, and access provisions. In addition to these standard practices, the DPRK must also account for the over 20,000 metric tons of food left behind when the DPRK expelled U.S. food monitors in March 2009.

———

RESPONSES OF ASSISTANT SECRETARY OF STATE KURT CAMPBELL TO QUESTIONS SUBMITTED BY SENATOR JOHN F. KERRY

*Question.* Some observers have asked whether North Korea policy has taken a back seat to the wars in Afghanistan and Iraq, the Iranian nuclear challenge, and the Middle East peace process, to say nothing of pressing domestic and international economic priorities. In recent weeks, our foreign policy establishment is justifiably focused on the monumental developments still unfolding in the Middle East.

- Given the crowded international and domestic agenda, what priority do you attach to securing peace and stability on the Korean Peninsula?
- Have the recent disclosures of North Korea's uranium enrichment program made North Korea an even more pressing concern?

Answer. Maintaining peace and stability on the Korean Peninsula and the Asia-Pacific region and achieving the verifiable denuclearization of the Korean Peninsula in a peaceful manner remain key U.S. foreign policy priorities.

We have long suspected North Korea of having a uranium enrichment capability, and we have regularly raised it with the North Koreans and with our partners. North Korea's claim to have a uranium enrichment program (UEP) is yet another provocative act and, if true, contradicts its own pledges and commitments under the 2005 Joint Statement of the Six-Party Talks and its obligations under U.N. Security Council Resolutions 1718 and 1874. The construction of uranium enrichment facilities, as well as any related activity, is unacceptable and inconsistent with the objective of the verifiable denuclearization of the Korean Peninsula, which has long been the core goal of the six-party talks.

North Korea's UEP disclosure underscores the threat that its nuclear and ballistic missile programs and proliferation activities pose to global security. We urge the international community to implement U.N. Security Council Resolutions 1718 and 1874 fully and transparently. We continue to coordinate with our allies and partners to determine an appropriate response to the DPRK UEP, including at the U.N.

*Question.* The wider area around the South Korean-North Korean border is among the most militarized, if not the most militarized, in the world. Last year tensions reached the highest level in decades as a result of North Korea's provocative behavior.

- Is the Obama administration concerned by the potential for miscalculation or inadvertence producing a wider scale conflict?
- What steps is the Obama administration taking in concert with our South Korean ally to preserve stability and minimize the possibility of miscalculation or misunderstanding resulting in wider scale conflict?

Answer. Following the DPRK's sinking of the *Cheonan,* its disclosure of a uranium enrichment program, and its shelling of Yeonpyong Island, the United States has engaged in intensive diplomatic activities and policy coordination with the ROK and our other Five-Party partners. Our actions have ensured clear communication, preserved regional stability, and resulted in a constructive strategy for the way forward on North Korea. The United States and the ROK continue to routinely conduct joint military exercises to enhance interoperability and the readiness of alliance forces to respond to threats to peace.

--------

RESPONSES OF DR. MARCUS NOLAND TO QUESTIONS SUBMITTED BY
SENATOR JOHN F. KERRY

FOOD AID

The U.N. World Food Programme (WFP), which is responsible for much of the food aid in North Korea, has reportedly said its current food supply could sustain operations in the North for only another month. Next month, the WFP plans to complete its assessment of North Korea's food situation. But not many doubt that North Korea's 24 million people need more food, and I note your observation that the situation appears to be "deteriorating" once again and also that early spring historically has often been a more challenging period in terms of food security.

*Question.* It's imperative that international food aid reach hungry North Korean children and their families—not the military and supporters of the regime. Is it possible to take effective measures to limit the diversion of food assistance and, if so, what can be done?

Answer. Diversion is a real and troubling phenomenon. The fundamental issue is that the North Korean Government has never "bought in" to internationally accepted norms regarding humanitarian aid. In this context there are three strategies that we can pursue to inhibit diversion or limit its negative impact.

First, we need to implement the most rigorous monitoring program possible. In 2005, the World Food Programme (WFP) touted an agreement reached "in principle" with the North Korean Government that would mark an enormous improvement in the monitoring regime:

- Household food information. Every 4 months the WFP would undertake baseline household surveys, interview local officials and others (e.g., farmers, factory officials), hold focus group discussions, and take observational walks. The first household survey was conducted in June 2005.
- Distribution monitoring. The WFP would shift at the margin to monitoring distribution centers and food-for-work projects, interview those receiving food aid there, and increase monitoring visits to nonhousehold sites (e.g., county warehouses, factories producing food products with WFP commodities, institutions receiving food aid).
- Ration cards. All WFP beneficiaries would be given a WFP-designed and printed ration card that would be checked by WFP at distributions. As of August 2005, the distribution of these cards was nearly complete.
- Commodity tracking. WFP staff would be allowed to physically follow food aid from the port of entry, to county warehouses, to three to six Public Distribution Centers (PDCs) per county, as well as implement a more uniform and consistent system to track commodities by waybill number, with the ultimate goal of eventually introducing an electronic system that would allow tracking of individual

bags from port to final point of delivery. The first visits to PDCs began in June 2005.

This program was never implemented. Increased bilateral assistance and an improved harvest provided the North Koreans the opportunity to backtrack.

The issue was rejoined in 2007–08 when the U.S. Government agreed to provide up to 500,000 metric tons of grain, partially through the WFP and partially through a consortium of U.S. nongovernmental organizations (NGOs). The NGOs did not adopt the full technological package that the WFP had laid out in 2005 but did appear to make improvements in monitoring over previous practices, by using Korean speakers in-country for instance, something that had been previously prohibited. The WFP appears to have forgotten the 2005 agreement; reverted to earlier, weaker monitoring protocols; and was ultimately unable to mount a credible program to deliver the slated aid.

The 2005 agreement in principle stands as one benchmark, the monitoring regime implemented by the NGOs in 2008 another. Any monitoring program should try to go beyond these.

Even in the best circumstances, however, there is likely to be diversion. But it is important to keep in mind and exploit the reality that even if diverted, aid does not just disappear into the ether: Someone consumes it. In this regard, there are two strategies that we can pursue to limit the deleterious impact of aid diversion.

First, some forms of aid are more prone to diversion than others. Among bulk grains, rice is preferred for elite consumption; corn is less preferred, and barley and millet are the least preferred. If we are going to provide aid in the form of bulk grains, it would be better to provide it in forms that are not preferred for elite consumption. Even if diverted and monetized, the grain will likely be consumed by poor people.

Likewise, we should target aid delivery into the worst affected regions, a policy USAID first began in 2005. The logic is of the second-best: Even if the aid is diverted as it enters the country, it is likely to pool in that catchment area and be sold in markets in the worst affected regions; while it would be best for a aid to reach the narrowly targeted population, like the case of providing aid in less preferred forms, even if sold it is likely to be sold to a needy population.

Finally, one should be careful in thinking about delivery of specialized infant formulas or other therapeutic products; these may be highly susceptible to diversion and potentially fatal if administered incorrectly.

*Question.* What impact do you think food aid has on the Kim government's control over the economy?

*Answer.* On the whole, aid almost surely benefits the state. The issue is how one weighs that implication against the amelioration of suffering. The impact of aid on political control (and ultimately economic control) is partly a function of how the aid is delivered and, as in the case of diversion, there is a hierarchy of approaches in terms of their susceptibility to misuse. Direct delivery to targeted populations such as infants or pregnant women is the most preferred; the nature of the target and delivery method would seem largely to insulate this approach from politicization.

Bulk aid delivered through the public distribution system (PDS) reinforces government control: It comes through a state-controlled channel, the public pays money to the government to receive it, and the source of the aid can be obscured. (When the end-user receives the aid at a PDC, it literally comes in bulk form through a chute; the consumer does not see any bag with a U.S. flag or source information.) In the past the government has given certain groups, such as workers at state-owned enterprises, preferential access to the PDS (and hence aid), indirectly tying access to food to loyalty to state institutions.

However, there are other forms of delivery that are less susceptible to misuse. One is work-for-food projects in which people engage in work (typically on infrastructural projects). This approach is subject to state capture (the state can choose the project and workers), but the aid is less prone to outright diversion and is probably less effective in reinforcing state power than delivery of bulk grains through the PDS.

*Question.* Can international food assistance help fuel the growth of private markets in North Korea?

*Answer.* Ironically, international food aid has fueled the growth of private markets in North Korea. During the famine period of the 1990s, the real price of food was extraordinarily high. Control of aid potentially conveyed astronomical rents—but only if markets existed where these rents could be monetized and captured. The entry of large scale aid into North Korea in the mid-1990s created an incentive within at least parts of the elite—the military, for example—to allow the development of markets as a platform for personal or group enrichment. Aid was essentially a lubricant in the creation of markets. Diverted aid, which we seek to limit for policy reasons, presumably continues to play this role.

The conterminous existence of markets and aid contributes to a symbiotic relationship between market participants and PDS managers (who in some cases appear be one and the same) and the political structure more generally. Middlemen need to know when aid shipments are likely to arrive and push down prices, nationally and locally. In such a situation it is difficult to parse the overlapping interests between centrally placed officials, local PDS managers, and market participants. One thing we can say is that aid creates greater price volatility in the market (since it can represent a large increment of marginal supply) and works against the interests of cultivators since it depresses prices for their output.

## POLITICAL IMPLICATIONS OF ECONOMIC STRUGGLES

You have described how state failure in the North Korean economy has led to the spread of market activities that may represent "semiautonomous zone(s) of social communication and, potentially, political organizing.

*Question.* Does this development point to the prospect of near term political instability in your view?

*Answer.* Given the dearth of civil society institutions in North Korea capable of channeling mass discontent into constructive political action, I am skeptical that the apparent increased personal autonomy associated with the development of markets and new forms of communication such as cell phones has proceeded to an extent that it augurs political instability in the near term. This is a long-term process that I do believe will impose increasing constraints on the government, admittedly beginning from a point of near complete unaccountability. In the near term, reforms are more likely to emerge from intraelite competition following the death of Kim Jong-il than from a ground up movement.

*Question.* Are there ways that you think the United States and the international community should position itself vis-a-vis the North Korean people to leverage what you describe as the state failure of the North Korean economy?

*Answer.* The rehabilitation of North Korea's failing economy poses two interrelated challenges. The first is to raise per capita incomes to address the country's widespread poverty and food insecurity. The second is to encourage a fundamental reorientation away from the state and toward effectively functioning market-oriented institutions. The latter has a political dimension as well: Apart from improving the functioning of the economy and better addressing the population's material needs, the development of more market-oriented institutions, even if not fully independent of state control, would ameliorate the pervasive control over people's lives.

However, we cannot assume that any and all forms of economic engagement will have similarly transformative effects. To the extent that North Koreans have any interactions with foreigners, it is often with government agencies or NGOs. Given the North Korean milieu, it is quite natural for North Koreans to think of such engagement as a form of political bargaining. But an important long-run task of engagement is a sort of political-economic socialization: to educate North Koreans about the functioning of market economics and to reorient their conception of engagement away from politically driven resource transfers or political tribute and toward mutually beneficial exchange. The transformative potential of external economic integration will depend crucially on the nature of the economic ties that develop between North Korea and its partners and the extent to which such ties can be appropriated by politically connected groups such as the Kim family clique, the party, and/or the military.

In such a context, not all forms of public and private engagement are equally transformative. One can imagine a hierarchy of modalities of engagement that combine public involvement with private investment and trade, each with differential effects on the long-run objective of reform. From the standpoint of encouraging systemic transformation in North Korea, energy pipelines or even transportation links would have the least impact. Next in this hierarchy would be projects such as Mt. Kumgang, which can literally and figuratively be fenced off from the rest of the North Korean economy and society and as a result have limited effects on institutional transformation. Industrial parks, bonded warehouses, and other preferential investment zones in urban areas would be preferable, and investment by foreign firms throughout North Korea would be the best of all. Sadly, it is apparent that Pyongyang understands the implications of these different modalities of engagement and prefers precisely the ones that generate hard currency earnings without requiring significant alteration of existing practices.

Yet even under the most propitious conditions, it is evident that the government will attempt to steer economic engagement through state-controlled entities rather than the emerging nonsanctioned market-based actors our surveys documented. One implication is the necessity of developing Sullivan-type principles of labor standards, similar to those implemented by U.S. investors during the apartheid period in South Africa, to ensure that foreign investors do more than simply exploit virtual slave-labor conditions. For investors from South Korea, Japan, the United States, and other Organization for Economic Cooperation and Development (OECD) members, adherence to the OECD's Guidelines for Multinational Enterprises, including those ensuring that North Korean workers are aware of their rights and how to exercise them, would be another way of trying to ameliorate the impact that engagement with state-owned entities in North Korea could have in terms of reinforcing state control.

### VIEWS OF NORTH KOREAN PEOPLE

Given the tight political and social control exerted by the North Korean Government, we have very little insight into the everyday lives of North Koreans and the nature of their relationship with their government. Through the extensive interviews conducted by experts like you and Barbara Demick, we have begun to acquire some insight into their situations.

*Question.* How did most of the over 1,600 North Korean refugees you interviewed for your recent book seem to view the North Korean Government while they were living in North Korea?

Answer. In a strict sense this question is impossible to answer because no one has been able to interview North Koreans while they were in North Korea; our knowledge is based on self-reported retrospective statements by refugees about their beliefs while in North Korea, which are almost impossible to verify and subject to recollection bias. And, there are differences between people. That said, on the whole, the attitudes of the survey respondents might be summarized as follows. If asked while in North Korea, the "approval rating" that they would have generated would have been low. However, their understanding of life beyond North Korea was incomplete and subject to huge gaps in knowledge, some filled by myth and rumor. Once outside North Korea—even in China, which we tend to think of as a less than fully free information environment—as they began to learn more about the outside world, North Korea's position in it, and by extension the relative situation of loved ones left behind, their attitudes harden further, at least at the margin.

*Question.* While living in North Korea, did many of the refugees you interviewed seem to subscribe to the regime's central narrative that hostile foreign forces are to be blamed for the country's problems?

Answer. Again, it is impossible to fully verify these self-reported retrospective accounts. Nevertheless, it appears that an implication of increasing access to nonstate news sources has contributed to growing skepticism about the regime's central narrative. Over time, the share of respondents who blamed foreigners for their situation steadily fell, and the numbers who held their own government responsible formed a large majority.

*Question.* Do you see signs that within the next 5 years, civil society voices might emerge capable of channeling dissent into effective political action?

Answer. I would be very modest about my ability to divine such developments. There may be developments occurring beneath the surface or that outsiders don't fully grasp that could give rise to some kind of civil society voice that does not currently exist. I am thinking, for example, of student or professional groups, or even public employee networks that bring together people from different parts of the country, create opportunities for "comparing notes"—both within and beyond their prescribed mandate, and could possibly serve as a mechanism for group action across localities. I don't know that such networks exist, but I would not be surprised if they do, and their political relevance is unpredictable. Also perhaps not precisely analogous in terms of their political implications, former United Kingdom Ambassador John Everard argues that the supply networks that bring goods from China to Pyongyang constitute an important informational network, bringing people information about the outside world and news of developments both inside and outside of North Korea not provided through official channels.

*Question.* Based on your conversations with refugees, what policy initiatives might contribute most toward increasing North Koreans' knowledge and awareness of developments inside and outside their country?

Answer. I think that there is a lot of role for exchanges; even if the groups are hand-picked by the government, and even if there are minders within these groups, there must be some value to getting larger numbers of North Koreans out into the world and interacting with foreigners.

The refugees say that while they were in North Korea they liked listening to foreign radio broadcasts. One of the most rewarding experiences I have ever had was after a talk that I had given in Seoul being introduced to a young North Korean refugee graduate student who had been in the audience and asked a mutual acquaintance for an introduction. She told me that when she was in North Korea she used to listen to my interviews on Radio Free Asia because I made the economic developments within her country comprehensible—something that the state was unwilling to do. There are people listening.

---

RESPONSES OF L. GORDON FLAKE TO QUESTIONS SUBMITTED BY
SENATOR JOHN F. KERRY

### NORTH-SOUTH DYNAMICS

*Question.* Tensions on the Korean Peninsula remain high after the shelling of Yeonpyeong Island. The North's recent behavior raises the distinct possibility of further destabilizing conduct in 2011 and has significantly hardened official views in Seoul.

- Is the present situation significantly more dangerous than what we have seen in recent years?

Answer. Yes; it is. The most important factor in this is the change in South Korea's willingness to respond to North Korean provocations with force. Not only has South Korea significantly revised its rules of engagement for responding to North Korean actions, but President Lee Myung Bak is now politically in a position where should he fail to respond to a similar provocation he could very well face severe political consequences. After the North Korean shelling of Yeongpyeong Island in November there were already calls from some corners of the Presidents own party for his impeachment for having failed to protect the nation. It is unclear that the North Korean leadership understands this change in South Korea, and as such the situation is dangerous indeed.

- What are the risks that South Korea and our alliance faces should Seoul fight back against a future North Korean attack?

Answer. The most obvious risk is the one we have lived with for nearly 60 years, the specter of another full scale war on the Korean Peninsula. Though by most estimates, North Korean no longer possesses a serious invasive capacity and absent outside assistant does not have the ability to sustain a conflict, with its long range artillery, its missiles, chemical and biological weapons and possibly a nuclear device, Pyongyang does have the ability to hold Seoul hostage and to make any conflict, regardless of the ultimate outcome, indescribably costly. Our South Korean allies know this far better than we do and feel the implications much more directly. As such I do not think that we need to be overly worried about South Korea dragging us into a conflict. In fact, should the United States appear to be holding South Korea back—as we did in the years immediately after the signing of the armistice—in the face of such egregious North Korea provocations, such perceptions could undermine South Korean views of the reliability of the United States as an ally when most needed. That said, perhaps the greatest risk that the United States and the Republic of Korea jointly face is that North Korea would be unable to calibrate its counter-response to a South Korean response and that communication channels with and within North Korea would not be sufficient to prevent a full scale escalation.

### CHINA'S ROLE/IMPLICATIONS FOR U.S. POLICY

*Question.* You have recently written about China's efforts "to shield[] North Korea from the consequences of its actions." Senior government officials have used words such as "enabled" and "emboldened" to discuss the impact of China's tolerance of North Korea's aggressive conduct. Any effort to wait out North Korea by increasing pressure, withholding economic benefits, and dangling the prospect of large-scale aid and diplomatic benefits in return for fundamentally different behavior would seem to require enhanced Chinese cooperation.

• Is China, over time, willing to make this kind of a shift in approach?

Answer. While I am hopeful that over time, China will be willing to recalibrate its approach to North Korea, recent events in the Middle East have increased China's own sense of vulnerability and thus reinforced the most conservative elements in the Chinese leadership. As such, at least for the next year or so it is difficult to imaging China taking steps which might raise the risk of instability in North Korea. In the longer term, however, North Korea's actions and trajectory are so fundamentally antithetical to China's own direction and national interest that some shift in China's approach to North Korea is inevitable.

• How much do concerns about Northeast Asia realigning in ways that run counter to China's interests (in response to North Korean behavior) influence Beijing's thinking?

Answer. I am no longer convinced by the conventional argument that China needs North Korea as a "buffer." While China would be concerned about U.S. troops North of the 38th parallel, by almost any measure, China's interests and positions are far better aligned with a modern South Korea than with its troublesome and anachronistic ally North Korea. Furthermore, North Korea's actions have actually served to bolster the U.S.–ROK alliance, the United States-Japan alliance, and even nascent security cooperation between South Korea and Japan. It is hard to imagine a scenario in which fundamental change in North Korea and the related realignment of Northeast Asia could be worse for China's interest.

• How much have concerns in Beijing about such a realignment contributed to a tighter Chinese embrace of North Korea over the past year?

Answer. Although it may be a factor, I think it is misguided. Moreover, I think the primary factor behind China's tighter embrace of North Korea has less to do with long-term concerns about regional realignment and more to do with immediate concerns about the stability of the Kim regime.

JAPAN'S ROLE

*Question.* In recent months, our ally Japan has taken noticeable steps to show solidarity with the United States and South Korea after a tense year on the Korean Peninsula. For the first time, Tokyo sent observers to U.S.–ROK military exercises in November and later announced plans to develop closer security cooperation with South Korea. In December, a trilateral summit to discuss the situation on the Peninsula confirmed Japan's strong support for a unified response to the North. What do these welcomed developments say about the way that Japan perceives the North Korean challenge?

Answer. The 1998 North Korean long-range missile test which flew over Japan served to make North Korea a focal point of Japanese public opinion. Furthermore, the tragic case of Japanese abductees has put a human face on the issue as felt by ordinary Japanese. In last year, the sinking of the *Cheonan* and the shelling of Yeonpyeong Island have served to further highlight the immediacy of the North Korean threat. As such, in terms of United States-Japan alliance coordination and cooperation, North Korea is the gift that keeps on giving. One other element that should be understood is that for Japan, North Korea is also increasingly tied up in the broader question of China's rise and role in the region. The naval class near the Senkaku/ Diaoyu islands last year brought security concerns about China to the fore in an unprecedented manner. As such, as matters develop it is likely that Japan will increasingly view the North Korea issue in the context of Chinese support for North Korea.

————

RESPONSES OF ROBERT CARLIN TO QUESTIONS SUBMITTED BY
SENATOR JOHN F. KERRY

NORTH KOREAN POLITICS: REGIME STABILITY AND LEADERSHIP SUCCESSION

You are one of this country's most experienced North Korea watchers. Even prior to Kim Jong-il succeeding his father Kim Il-Sung in 1994, analysts have been predicting the collapse of the North Korean Government. We are still waiting and rightly planning for potential changes to come.

*Question.* In your written testimony, you say, however that "[i]t does not make sense to base a policy on the assumption that a collapse will happen soon—that is, in the next 2–3 years." Why, and what are the dangers of laboring under such an assumption?

Answer. Many like to think we can assess the health and expected longevity of political systems with an approach similar to what doctors use for living beings. Political science delights in charts and graphs to plot "regime health" and predict collapse. In truth, the track record is much better in identifying the warning signs after the event than in advance.

Over the past 30 years, we've been through numerous episodes when analysts predicted the end was nigh for the DPRK. North Korea is still with us.

There have been several times when some in Washington convinced themselves that the North was near or on the road to collapse. These officials have moved on; Pyongyang is still a going concern.

The problem with basing a policy on the assumption that North Korean collapse is around the corner is that it leads us down any one of several dead-end roads, convincing us to: sit patiently on our haunches and do nothing; adopt a shortsighted approach designed to chase after the will-o'-wisp of collapse; or make unrealistic commitments that one hopes will never have to be met because the North will disappear before the bill comes due. The result in each case is that the situation grows worse, the problem more complicated. The only constant is the refrain from Washington, "What do we do now?" Once it's too late, what we can't do is to go back and take those steps that might have protected U.S. national interests at an earlier point but have now been overtaken by events.

*Question.* You also warn that if and when social and political unrest occurs in the North, it could "quickly descend into violence that could make Libya look like a tea party." Why, and what are the implications of this statement for U.S. policy?

Answer. The North has a large army and numerous security forces, huge quantities of weapons with a population trained to use them, and enough loyalists to ensure that any sort of internal fighting will be intense. In such a situation, the United States will find itself in a dangerous position. Unlike in Libya, where external forces have been able to act with relative impunity under the mantle of a U.N. resolution, in the case of North Korea both China and Russia will almost certainly block a similar sort of mandate. A "no fly zone" over the DPRK—especially given the fact that several major North Korean cities are either on the border or less than 20 miles from China—is out of the question for Beijing. The result will very likely be a lengthy, destructive, and destabilizing internal conflict right on the doorstep of our treaty allies: the ROK and Japan. In those circumstances, to the extent Seoul feels it can or must influence the outcome, that will only add fuel to the fire and put enormous strains on U.S.-ROK relations.

*Question.* There appears to be increasingly little question that Kim Jong-il's youngest son Kim Jong-un is being groomed to succeed his father. What are your observations with regard to how the succession process is proceeding in North Korea? What are the implications for regional peace and security?

Answer. From the point that Kim Jong-un was formally revealed in public (certainly to the external audience) in September 2010, the succession process has appeared to move quickly and smoothly. Since we don't know for sure when the process actually began for the internal audience, however, we can't very well say whether it is ahead of schedule or moving at a forced pace.

Perhaps the better questions to ask are whether the younger Kim yet has a cadre of his own loyalists in place, how much experience he has had or still needs in key positions in the party's Central Committee, and whether he has the intestinal fortitude to rule. Obviously, a botched succession raises the dangers of the sort of situation discussed above. Some observers believe that the succession process itself brings with it a period of uncertainty and a likelihood of increased tensions (not to mention military clashes) as the successor seeks to win his spurs and those around him act to prove their loyalty. This is the stuff of TV drama, but I don't know of any evidence that it is actually the case in North Korea. Rather than look on the succession only as a period of heightened danger, it makes as much sense for the U.S. to view it as a time of opportunity, a period when it becomes possible to search for new openings and, with equal measures of luck and perseverance, to create new realities less dangerous, more manageable, and hopefully more amenable to our own national security interests.

### NORTH KOREA: MOTIVATIONS AND THREAT PERCEPTIONS

*Question.* Within the past year, North Korea has sunk the ROK frigate *Cheonan,* shelled Yeonpyeong Island, announced a clandestine uranium enrichment facility to the world, and, according to recent reports, readied a second missile launch facility that might be capable of launching long-range missiles. Despite these developments, you wrote in your testimony that "North Korea is largely in deterrent-defensive mode—militarily, diplomatically, and in every other way." How does this square with widely held perceptions of the North's recent behavior, and who and what does Pyongyang feel the need to deter/defend against?

Answer. The North Koreans have a siege mentality, as well they might. They see themselves as inhabiting a small, weak country put upon and threatened on all sides, with not a single, solitary reliable ally. Small countries that survive over time usually do so by adopting one of two basic postures toward their larger neighbors— bended knee or hedgehog. The North has chosen the latter. Its prickliness is not just with the United States, but also with the PRC and, when it existed, the USSR. The Wilson Center's "Cold War History" series of documents illustrate for anyone interested just how exasperating the North has long been to friend and foe alike.

It is worth bearing in mind that the North is not an expansionist power and has no territorial ambitions outside the Korean Peninsula. How serious it even continues to pursue reunification is an open question. I think the evidence suggests it hasn't had much stomach for a military solution to that question for at least 30 years. Instead, the two Koreas have settled into a long, sometimes violent, political struggle. By virtue of its political vitality and economic success, South Korea is much more of a threat to the North's existence than the other way around. The result is that the North—by far the weaker party—feels it imperative to push back, keep the South off balance, and continuously assert its right to survive. Sometime this takes the form of diplomatic initiatives, sometimes of limited military moves. In Pyongyang's view, nothing could be worse than a peace and quiet in which the world could forget that North Korea exists. The greatest danger for the past 20 years has not been a large-scale North Korean military move against the South but a small military incident spiraling into something bigger and more dangerous. The North's shelling of Yeonpyeong Island, as bad as it was, seemed to bring us very close to the threshold of something much worse. Indeed, the situation in the West Sea—with conflicting North-South Korean claims and escalating military reinforcements by both sides—is more and more a powder keg.

## CHINA'S ROLE

*Question.* In your written testimony, you warn against "sitting and waiting while another country shape[s] the future of Northeast Asia." Can you elaborate on this statement and its implications for peace and stability on the Korean Peninsula?

Answer. North Korea is not the jewel in the crown, but how the Korean issue is eventually resolved will help set the stage for developments in Northeast Asia for decades to come. There was a time not so long ago when the United States had an active, not simply reactive, policy toward North Korea. Washington's leadership on the issue made it easier for both Japan and South Korea (to the extent they chose to do so) to engage Pyongyang. There was impressive, ongoing coordination between Tokyo, Seoul, and Washington on a positive program to deal with the North. And, wonder of wonders, Pyongyang was a willing participant because it saw establishing a positive relationship with the United States as a way to retain maximum independence from its big neighbor across the Yalu River.

The situation today is completely different, and dangerously so. Under any circumstances we know that China will insist on—and must have—a voice in eventual resolution of the Korean question. But these days the Chinese role has been magnified as the United States has removed itself from any serious dealings with the DPRK. With nothing standing in its way, China seems to be moving to insure that the weight and breadth of its presence in North Korea—and by extension its influence on the entire peninsula—will only grow larger and more permanent in the future.

That doesn't augur well for peace and stability either in Korea or the region. I do not mean this as a criticism of China, nor should it be taken to imply that we must be suspicious of Chinese motives. It is a simple fact, however, that the United States still has treaty commitments as well as important economic and political interests that demand our full-time involvement in Korea—the whole of Korea. Absent our serious, sustained, and effective involvement on the peninsula, the impression will grow that ours is no longer the vital presence in the area. Military exercises and displays of armed might only go so far. By themselves, they cannot overcome the dangerous notion—and let's not fool ourselves, such a notion is afoot—that the United States is a waning power, at least in Northeast Asia, and that China's star is rising. The expanding Chinese presence in North Korea, we should reckon, may come to symbolize the new day, demonstrating China's growing ability to shape the future on a crucial regional issue in a way, some will argue, that the United States no longer seeks to do.

RESPONSES OF SPECIAL REPRESENTATIVE STEPHEN BOSWORTH AND ASSISTANT SECRETARY KURT CAMPBELL TO QUESTIONS SUBMITTED BY SENATOR MIKE LEE

*Question.* In light of the past year, which has been a tense one for North Korean relations with South Korea and the United States, (North Korea torpedoed and sank the South Korean *Cheonan,* directly attacked South Korea and announced new nuclear facilities) do you stand by the Obama administration's policy of "strategic patience"?

Answer. The Obama administration has made clear from the start that there is a path open to North Korea to achieve the security and international respect it seeks and that we are open to serious dialogue with North Korea on denuclearization. However, this process depends on the decisions and actions of North Korea. We are looking for evidence that North Korea now not only regards the possibility of negotiations seriously but also that such negotiations could be constructive. We want negotiations to achieve the core goal of the 2005 joint statement: the verifiable denuclearization of the Korean Peninsula in a peaceful manner. We are not interested in negotiations for the sake of talking.

We do not believe it will be fruitful or productive to resume six-party talks until North Korea demonstrates it is committed to dialogue and serious about honoring its denuclearization commitments. We believe the DPRK must improve North-South relations and demonstrate a change in behavior, including ceasing provocative actions, taking steps toward irreversible denuclearization, and complying with its commitments under the 2005 Joint Statement of the Six-Party Talks and its obligations under U.N. Security Council Resolutions 1718 and 1874.

*Question.* What evidence, if any, have you seen indicating that the third prong of "strategic patience" (a gradual altering of China's relationship with North Korea) has come to pass?

Answer. China is a vital partner in the six-party talks with a key role due to its influence with North Korea. Given its unique relationship with North Korea, we have called on China to urge the DPRK to refrain from provocative actions, to abide by its commitments and obligations, and to act responsibly in the interests of peace and stability of the Northeast Asian region. In the United States-China Joint Statement from President Hu Jintao's January 19–20 state visit, both countries "expressed concern regarding the DPRK's claimed uranium enrichment program," "opposed all activities inconsistent with the 2005 Joint Statement and relevant international obligations and commitments," and "called for the necessary steps that would allow for the early resumption of the six-party talks process to address this and other relevant issues."

*Question.* How closely does the State Department work with the U.S. Department of Defense in North Korean relations? I understand that the United States has about 30,000 troops stationed in South Korea. What is the plan to increase U.S. military presence if/when necessary?

Answer. The Department of State and Department of Defense work together closely to maintain and strengthen our robust military alliance with the ROK in our mission of defending the ROK and deterring North Korean aggression. Our military is prepared to deal with many different scenarios and can bring many capabilities to bear.

*Question.* What evidence, if any, have you seen to suggest that Kim Jong-un could emerge as a reformer in North Korea, and one who might be open to political and social reform?

Answer. North Korea is one of the world's most closed societies, so it is difficult to predict the future of the North Korean regime. We are carefully watching the situation in Pyongyang, especially as Kim Jong-un, Kim Jong-il's third son and heir apparent, advances within the regime's hierarchy.

*Question.* The relatively peaceful revolt (and hopefully subsequent democratization) in Egypt began with and spread partly because of prodemocracy messages sent via the Internet and social media outlets. What access do the average North Korean people have to outside media?

Answer. The DPRK government tightly controls the media and its citizens' access to information. The State Department's "2009 Country Reports on Human Rights Practices" notes that there is no independent media in North Korea and Internet access in North Korea is limited to high-ranking officials and other designated elites. However, the U.S. Government is working to increase the flow of independent information into, out of, and within the country. The Broadcasting Board of Governors supports a robust North Korea program, implemented by the Voice of America and Radio Free Asia. In addition, the Department of State supports nongovernmental organizations in their efforts to increase access to information in North Korea, including support to independent broadcasters based in South Korea.

*Question.* How active has Russia been in diplomatic discussions regarding North Korea or in military support and training for South Korea?

Answer. We value our continuing cooperation with Russia, a key partner in the six-party talks, to achieve our shared goal of denuclearization in North Korea. In the wake of the DPRK's provocations over the last year, we welcome the constructive role that Russia has played to press Pyongyang to refrain from further destabilizing actions, to abide by its international commitments and obligations, and to take irreversible steps toward denuclearization. Russia has publicly stated that it backs U.N. Security Council discussion of the North Korean uranium enrichment program.

*Question.* In 1994, the United States and North Korea signed the Agreed Framework. Under this agreement, North Korea committed to freezing its illicit plutonium weapons program in exchange for aid.

- What benefits did the United States receive from the Agreed Framework?
- What is the current state of North Korea's plutonium weapons program?
- In short, what has the United States received from the hundreds of millions of dollars in aid we've given to North Korea?

Answer. As a result of the Agreed Framework of October 1994, North Korea halted construction of two large reactors and froze its existing plutonium production facilities at Yongbyon, including its reprocessing facilities, putting them under continuous monitoring by the International Atomic Energy Agency (IAEA). That continuously monitored freeze lasted for over 8 years until late 2002 and helped prevent what could have resulted in a much larger plutonium stockpile than North Korea is currently assessed to possess. Building on the results of the Agreed Framework process in 1999, the United States and North Korea also negotiated a moratorium on North Korean ballistic missile launches, which stayed in effect until 2006.

North Korea announced on April 14, 2009, its withdrawal from the six-party talks, the expulsion of IAEA monitors and U.S. disablement experts, and its intention to reverse disablement actions taken at the Yongbyon nuclear complex. Since then, according to official statements issued by the DPRK, many of the disablement tasks completed between November 2007 and April 2009 have been reversed. For example, in November 2009, the DPRK announced that it had completed reprocessing 8,000 spent nuclear fuel roads at Yongbyon in August 2009. However, these claims have not independently been verified.

For over 8 years under the Agreed Framework, North Korea was prevented from making weapons grade plutonium. With the Agreed Framework's collapse, North Korea restarted the reactor and separated plutonium three times—enough for several weapons, as well as the devices it announced it had tested in 2006 and 2009. The prolonged disruption to the production of plutonium for North Korea's nuclear weapons program was a key tangible benefit of the Agreed Framework. In addition, the 1999 to 2006 moratorium on North Korean ballistic missile launches was a significant brake on its missile program.

○